MW00831874

Subtle
POWER

★

Unleash The Hidden Value Within

A Guide to the Human Operating System
for Intentional Leaders

★

Gabriel Sakakeeny

ISBN 978-0-9899251-1-2

First edition

Printed in the U.S.A.

Table of Contents

"The skillful are not obvious.

They appear to be simple-minded.

Those who know this know the patterns of the Absolute.

To know the patterns is the Subtle Power.

The Subtle Power moves all things and has no name."

– David R. Hawkins, Ph.D. M.D.

What If?

Is it possible for one person without celebrity, position, or connections to make a profound positive difference in the real-world business performance of a global corporation?

In 1999, a large multi-national high tech conglomerate spun off its under-performing test and measurement organization. By the end of 2003, after the .com bubble burst, the new company had suffered nine consecutive quarters of losses and multiple rounds of layoffs for the first time in its sixty-year history. The legacy culture of family relationship and graduation-to-retirement job security had been broken with its employees. The ranks of management were demoralized and dispirited, maneuvering opportunistically in an environment of cronyism, incompetent leadership, and chaotically mismanaged expectations.

In this depressed situation, one tactical level employee instigated a grass roots revival of key company values by designing and leading a cultural transformation packaged as an educational program for managers called CCR – Communication, Commitment, and Results – the precursor of the Leadership, Creativity, and Power curriculum. In spite of initial resistance from the HR establishment, the CCR training's focus on reality-based communication,

accountability, self-empowerment, and effective collaboration gained support in the management ranks and eventually swept through the company at all levels.

In the new company's Asia sales organization, a lone HR
manager led a breakthrough project for an approximately
five hundred person sales team. Using what he learned
in the program, he started what became a cultural
synchronization between sales teams in Korea, China,
Japan, Singapore, and the whole Asia/Pacific region. By
creating a powerful context of meaning, integrity, and
respect in the sales force, he and his executive sponsor
were able to lift the previously lackluster performance of
the Asia sales team to beyond predicted levels. In China,
sales results were fifteen percent (15%) over the targets.
In Korea, results exceeded the predictable by twenty-two
percent (22%). In Singapore and the rest of "Asia/Pacific,"
the results exceeded the predicted by 3.6 times! In addition
to these extraordinary sales results, the marketing team
more than doubled the amount of deals in the sales funnel.

In Northern California, a team of electronic engineers
in the new company's microwave test division used what
they learned about creating new thinking and implementing
creativity to rethink the process of manufacturing an
advanced, wide bandwidth, low noise microwave amplifier.
Before their breakthrough project began, each hand-made
amplifier took a total of 2.6 days to manufacture. After
applying what they learned, the team reduced the time
to manufacture to only 248 minutes – one-fifth the time.
Due to the increased output of their process and increased
reliability of the product, the team generated an additional
$10 million of value for the company in the first year.

Also in the Northern California region, a cross-functional team of managers from all parts of the new company was charged with implementing a new enterprise resource planning (ERP) system for the global enterprise. They used the reality-based methods of the CCR curriculum to reduce the time to plan the implementation from the predictable four months to two days. By learning how to distinguish results from the activities and processes that precede them, the team, in a two-day collaboration was able to clearly specify the thousands of physical results that were needed and then place those results in order on a timeline, bringing the "go-live" date forward by four months.

Other business units inside the new company took on the new methodology and replaced merely "being busy" with productivity, yielding millions of dollars of profit in a legacy environment of persistent loss. The leaders of those units were recognized as the new generation of high potential managers and were promoted based on their results. Eventually, the CEO and his top fifty executives took the CCR training and declared its methods the way forward for the company's future. With this executive level support, a body of trainers and coaches were hired to lead the program worldwide, eventually training over 3,300 managers and developing a multi-part curriculum of leadership development.

As a direct outcome of the leadership provided by that one tactical level employee, the management recovered their hope for the future and turned the company around from years of persistent failure to regaining their place as the world leader in test and measurement.

The story above is true. How is that possible?

★

On the concluding day of one Leadership, Creativity, and Power training, during the final sharing of insights in the room, a financial professional was prompted to share his insight. He said, "I hadn't realized before that my pants are olive green."

At first, I thought that he was acting out as people sometimes do when they feel the need to diminish the space of possibility in the room. This particular man had been resistant and sometimes argumentative throughout the program. It would have been "more of the same" for him to poke fun at what was otherwise an inspiring conversation about the learning that had occurred.

Rather than call him out on the behavior I asked, "That doesn't sound like an insight, Bill. What do you mean exactly?"

He then shared this report. "When I woke up this morning something had changed. I've been wearing these pants for years. I always thought that they were gray. When I went to the closet this morning to put them on, I noticed that they looked different. They were clearly olive green. When I went down to breakfast, I noticed that my children looked different. I could see them more clearly and their voices sounded more vivid and alive. When I kissed my wife as I was leaving the house, there was a moment of connection that had been a distant memory. Somehow I am more alive and more present than I can remember and this is because of the work we've been doing. Thank you."

The story above is true. How is that possible?

★

A small, 1,000-employee oil company based in Calgary, Alberta, had been struggling for several years. Each annual planning cycle, they set what they thought were realistic goals for exploration, drilling, production, and other business milestones. Then, during each quarterly review, the managers in charge of the various functions of the company reported missing their targets. The reports of failure were always accompanied by detailed explanations of the extenuating circumstances, excusing and justifying the lack of performance.

Because the executives in charge were conventionally reasonable people, they elected to adjust the yearly targets down to account for the shortfall in the previous quarter, assuming that their plans were not as realistic as they originally thought. This downward adjusting had been going on for several years.

When the company's stock price plummeted to $3.30 per share after more than two years of consistent failure, consultants were called in to help. During the initial discovery process, it was found that the company was staffed with highly analytical engineers and scientists who were oriented to data, process, and technological solutions. Their primary values were hard work, long hours, and rigorous thinking. Business results and outputs of processes were strongly de-emphasized in favor of the design of the processes themselves and the activities that were done inside those processes. These cultural preferences were consistent up and down the management ranks.

An overall corporate initiative was implemented that provided management and employee trainings, consulting, and executive coaching in the areas of accountability, leadership, communication effectiveness, and outcomes-based thinking. The top executives were trained first and rigorously coached to shift their attention away from office politics, explanations, research, and process to tangible results and integrity between what was promised and what was delivered. The same trainings were given to consecutively lower levels of management cascading through the company down to the most tactical employees.

In addition to training, coaching, and consulting, the company's functional managers took on ambitious stretch goals for the coming year. Each breakthrough project had specific tangible measures that were displayed on large graphs showing promised and actual results against time. These displays were hung in the main atrium through which all employees had to walk as they came and left the workplace. The performance of each team was displayed in weekly granularity for all to see.

Within nine months, the company was not only reaching the goals in its normal business plan but also achieving the stretch goals that had been set as part of the breakthrough projects. It had gone from an under-performing, poorly led collection of analytical individuals to a high-performance team. Within four years, the company's value had quadrupled. A larger energy conglomerate acquired it at a thirty-five percent (35%) premium over its final stock valuation.

The story above is true. How is that possible?

★

Oberlin College has an unusual academic schedule that includes a one-month "Winter Term" during January. Each year, students and professors can take on special projects that are outside the normal flow of the curriculum. One year, the Oberlin College Conservatory of Music offered a Winter Term program called "From Fear to Freedom." Designed for performing artists, public speakers, and others who must perform in real time under pressure, the program promised to provide a method by which, with practice, students could end the grip of performance anxiety.

In the beginning of the opening five-day intensive, the enrolled students had difficulty standing at the front of the room and speaking for thirty seconds about themselves and why they had enrolled in the class. Musicians, dancers, actors, athletes, and speakers shared how their emotional and physiological reactions had limited them in their ability to perform at the level that they knew was possible.

In the ensuing five days, they were taught a model for the mind and were trained to use that model, bringing awareness to their automatic responses and their unconscious points of view, beliefs, and habits of thought. They were also given a framework for creating a purpose for performance that shifted their focus from self-absorption to serving others. After the five-day intensive, there was a two-week hiatus in which they were to prepare a performance to be given in the last week of the month at a class recital.

By the end of the five-day intensive, every student was able to confidently present to a large group: who they were, what they stood for, and what they were going to do about it. They were now free of the grip of performance anxiety. At the recital, they reported performing with far greater ease and satisfaction. Each person shared that he or she had the ability to manage his or her habitual self-defeating thoughts and emotions, and expressed the pleasure they experienced in giving a performance to the audience. The program made such a difference for some that they formed a student organization promoting transformational education on campus.

The story above is true. How is that possible?

It is possible to fundamentally shift the way a group of people perceives themselves, their lives, and their work. This book contains the basics of the framework of thinking and perceiving that allowed for all of the extraordinary results described above. The upgrade in performance that occurs is predictable and repeatable across cultures, industry sectors, genders, and age groups. The result of installing that framework in an organization is a measurable increase in effectiveness on the order of 1.2 to 5 times, and a dramatic decrease in waste, drama, and fear among the workforce.

As in every creative endeavor, the manifestation of something truly new and real begins with a seed idea. While reading a book will not enable you to fully implement the framework in yourself or your own organization, it is our hope that being introduced to the ideas set forth here will open a new pathway in your thinking and perceiving that will enable you to plant the seed of effective action.

By reading this book, you will be able to consciously recognize what is driving you and your team's behaviors and the consequences that follow. Once those unseen motivators become conscious, it is only a matter of time before you will choose to do something with what you have learned.

Your leadership and your ability to cause an inspiring future is the subject of this book. We promise that by the end, you will see a new possibility for your self-expression and fulfillment as a creative leader in your business and your life.

Think On This

We have learned through experience that thoughts and ideas, when they are *only concepts*, often remain ephemeral in effect. But once you write your insights down on paper, they transform into something tangible: things with a physical existence that can manifest in reality, yielding actions and outcomes.[1]

With that in mind, this book is designed with blank pages at the end of each chapter *for your use* in recording your impressions, questions, thoughts, and most especially, discovered insights. This is your book and also the beginning journal of your progress in realizing proficiency in Leadership, Creativity, and Power. Please use this space; it

---

1   Mueller, P.A., and Oppenheimer, D.M. (in press). The Pen Is Mightier Than The Keyboard: Advantage of Longhand Over Laptop Notetaking. Psychological Science.

belongs to you. It is the springboard for your deep dive into your greatest potential.

If you are experiencing this as an e-book, please familiarize yourself with your annotation options, but better yet, begin a real journal in which to write down your insights. The act of putting pen to paper and *inscribing* is a powerful catalyst for your personal transformation and growth.

• Make it real; begin your insight journal now.

Everything written above is true. How is that possible? The information in this book was applied by the people who produced the results described above. It has created real value for thousands of people before you. To find out how, read on.

Insights

Insights

Preparing To Shift

To begin, let's get clear on the meaning of the word *leadership*. It's the sort of abstraction that everyone thinks they understand, but when questioned about it are hard pressed to make a clear distinction that leaves one with something solid.

So we can address the reality of your own leadership practice, we'll say that leadership is a personal ability. Just as marksmanship is the ability to hit a target with a projectile at a distance and musicianship is the ability to hear, read, write, and perform music, then *leadership is the ability to manifest the leader's intentions in reality with and through people.*

It's useful to talk about leadership as a personal ability because then we can relate it to the real world. It becomes measurable. Either you produced the intended outcome with your people, or you did not. We can make fact-based assessments about a person's leadership practice when the measures of it are a matter of physical, quantifiable results. It's not a matter of style, personality, or philosophy. It's not open to interpretation. It's a matter of your ability to accomplish something you intend with and through real people.

Most books, speeches, and trainings on leadership present models, platitudes, success stories, tips on what to avoid, best practices, and good habits to develop, all in an attempt to help you to increase the effectiveness of your leadership. Since leadership is something you do, not something you have or something you think, acquiring more information about leadership may have little to do with being able to get things done with people. Tips and tricks may be entertaining and provocative, but in the end, if you don't behave differently when it counts, your skill at leadership will not improve. It's possible to know a lot about leadership, talk a good game, even be a teacher of leadership, and yet remain completely incompetent at leading.

Why is this so? Knowing about things doesn't necessarily give you the ability to do them. Viewing skiing videos, reading about skiing, having a nice ski outfit, great skis and boots, a lift ticket, and talking about skiing does not give you the ability to ski. Now, if we take a skill that is much more complex than skiing, one that requires multifaceted interactions between human beings to get something accomplished, or having a long-term, deeply satisfying personal relationship with someone, or raising children who are ready for the world, we can see that knowing about these things, while helpful, is insufficient. A different kind of learning is required to develop the ability to create desired outcomes with and through other people. That's the difference between being interested in leadership and being able to manifest it.

While this book reveals insights and yields understanding of the principles of Leadership, Creativity, and Power, it is only *about* them. To actually *lead* from a position of creativity and power is a way of behaving. As we have suggested, *reading about* behavior, is not the same as *demon-*

strating it. You have to *live* the change and practice it in daily life for the learning to occur and to become part of your leadership skill set. Thus, when you have compared the principles in this book with your own life experiences and can judge their merit for yourself, you can choose to begin your voyage of mastery in them. Through generating and capturing your insights, you will open your thinking to the path ahead, one that leaves behind the waste, drama, and fear that permeates so many work environments. But to make the skills real and available to you as a leader, you need to train them in and to practice them in the real world. The only way to do this, in a reasonable amount of time and without trial and error, is to get trained by a professional who has mastered the skills and can teach others effectively. You will find information at the end of this book about how to begin your training in the LCP technology should you choose to do that.

Domains of Learning

To understand what kind of learning that might be, think with me for a minute, so that we can distinguish four different domains of learning. There is a domain of activites at which you are **consciously competent**. For instance, you may be a competent driver and know that. Or, you may be aware that you are competent at playing the cello. There are thousands of skills you have at which you are consciously competent.

There is also a domain of activities at which you are **consciously incompetent**. You may know that you are not a competent skier, for instance. If you want to become a competent skier, you know what to do – take lessons and practice until you have met your goal. Practice enables you to move from being incompetent to being competent. Your awareness and acceptance of your incompetence gives you the ability to choose to do the things required to become competent.

There is a very large domain comprised of skills at which you are **unconsciously incompetent**. Your ability level is unavailable for your conscious evaluation. It's not on the radar screen, even to consider. There are numerous skills like tuning oboe reeds, grading fine Chinese tea, or analyzing the intentional modality of speech, at which you have neither competence nor any knowledge of their existence. (Unless you do, of course!) But more insidious are the areas where we think we are competent, but when objectively measured, we are not. Consider someone who is tone deaf. He thinks he is singing quite well, but those listening can tell that he sounds musically incompetent. A person in this condition may strenuously make a case giving evidence for his competence, but from an external point of view using a defined set of standards against which to judge, he is clearly incompetent.

The problem in learning very complex skills, such as leadership, is that we are often unaware of our incompetence. If you don't know that you are incompetent, you can't choose to improve your ability because you are unaware that you even have a problem to begin with. You may have a delusional sense of your ability, thinking that you are better at leadership than you are in reality. You would then go through life unwittingly making the same mistakes, justifying and reasoning that your substandard results are caused by circumstances outside of yourself, even though others may be telling you otherwise (and ample evidence backs them up!)

To become competent at a skill, you first need to know and accept that you are incompetent. This will enable you to choose to take the actions needed to improve your ability. If you think you know it all already, you cannot learn. So the way you improve a skill that exists in the domain of unconscious incompetence is by working to make your incompetence conscious.

This sort of learning is usually unpopular with people who believe (or need to believe) that they are already successful. Like many who are in leadership positions, you may think that you are already pretty good at leading. You know yourself as a successful person. Your people seem to like you. Your contract keeps getting renewed. You may even be the best in your business at leading. You have a lot of "evidence" for your track record of successful leadership.

All that may be so, but if you wish to expand your ability to lead, you will have to look where you currently cannot see into the domain of your unconscious incompetence. That's because doing more of what you already know how to do is just going to give you more of what you've already got. If you want to elevate your skill to the next level, you must consciously and willfully seek out people and situations that will give you insight into your unwitting incompetence. This is not good news for your ego, but it is really great for your leadership practice and for those you serve by providing leadership!

> NOTE: Now would be a good time to take note of your thoughts, emotions, and body sensations.

Insight

An insight is a flash of awareness into something already present but not previously obvious. It occurs as a surprise – an "a-ha!" moment. Insights can be as mundane as stumbling across a feature you hadn't known about in a software application you use every day, or as profound as experientially realizing the true nature of your being. In every case, insights are new thoughts that make new possibilities of experience and action available. Noticing where you and others are not yet competent at leadership will generate insights that are relevant to developing your leadership ability.

Insights come from the courage and humility to tell the truth about your direct experiences and the creativity to generate insight from these experiences. Not everyone is ready to do this kind of work. Many of us would rather remain comfortably deluded than awake to what's really so about life and ourselves. Doing this work will require that you become comfortable with being uncomfortable from time to time. That is the price of winning new knowledge and skill.

Unlike most books on leadership, this one is designed to facilitate your generating insights into your nature as a human being who is leading other human beings. This book is written for those who are already producing results with and through other people on a daily basis. Executives, college presidents, leaders in the military, managers, facilitators, teachers, trainers, conductors, stage directors, clergy, choreographers, parents, and anyone else whose success is measured by the performance of people they lead will benefit most from this book.

We say that reality is the greatest teacher. The results will be the measure of your success. In this book, there will be little advice, few tips and techniques, and few entertaining stories *per se*. Through doing the work of generating insights, you will develop your own advice, tips, techniques, and stories that are uniquely appropriate and useful to you. Armchair leaders and readers, although welcome here, will likely not have enough at stake in the matter to do the hard work of mining their areas of unconscious incompetence. The value they receive will be proportional to the amount of skin they put in the game.

Have we scared you off? I hope not. Learning reality-based leadership is one of the most stimulating, interesting, and personally valuable disciplines I've ever engaged in. Doing this work has given me a self-determined life of joyous creativity, personal fulfillment, and ongoing growth and development. Out of doing the work, I have become fully myself, living true to my purpose in life in any circumstance. I am grateful for having been able to contribute to the success and fulfillment of thousands of people around the world whom I've had the privilege to lead in various settings over the years. I wish the same fulfillment and happiness for you.

Language is the method

The way we'll proceed in our work is by using language to create a rich lexicon of leadership. As we continue the work, your leadership vocabulary will get larger and the world of meaning that it generates will eventually turn into a detailed mental map that you can use to navigate the complexities of working with groups of people to produce extraordinary results.

This way of working is very similar to learning a foreign language. At first, you have a very small vocabulary that allows you to say "Please" and "Thank you," find the lavatory, and perhaps order at restaurants. As your vocabulary increases in size, the number of things you can think and communicate in the new language increases exponentially. You can eventually live, think, and dream in the new language world.

Some people try to learn new things by automatically critiquing everything they consider, reflexively finding fatal exceptions to every assertion, and critically arguing every new point as a way of trying to understand and integrate the new knowledge. If you are one of those, I want you to know that what follows is a discourse that yields a perspective, a new way of looking at the world that has proven over time to be very useful in developing leaders.

The ideas presented are not true in the sense that they refer to some independently existing referents out there in physical reality. Rather, they are a language system that allows people to think and perceive differently. These ideas are neither right nor wrong. They are a possible way to look at things. Thinking inside this vocabulary gives people new perspectives and insights into previously unconscious phenomena in the area of relationships, communication, and the creative process. Leading from inside this language yields measurably different results and activates dynamics that lead to success. And that is what we are about here.

Said differently, you won't be able to analyze enough to understand what will be presented. To get the value here, you will need to invent new thinking outside the frame that you already have in place. You will be synthesizing something new to you, not dissecting something that already exists.

For some people who have studied mathematics, learning calculus is a good example of this kind of approach to increasing the size of your mental framework. At some time in your life you did not know what integration and differentiation were. When your math professor first introduced the idea of adding together all those rectangles to calculate the area under the curve, the idea was foggy at best. You had to sit with it for a while and let it organize itself in your mind. You tried to understand it, but no matter how you tried to relate it to things you knew already, it just didn't become clear until, in a flash, the idea of integration suddenly made sense.

The same kind of thing happened when you first really understood the concept of imaginary numbers. When you created those ideas inside yourself, a new world of possibilities opened up for you in mathematics. The same thing will happen when you begin to create the vocabulary of leadership for yourself.

A useful concept for doing this kind of work is often called *beginner's mind* by practitioners of Zen Buddhism. If you are a beginner, you take the perspective that anything is possible. You don't know enough yet to know what is impossible or to even have formed a fixed opinion about the topic. Beginners are willing to try anything that their teacher suggests to them. As a result, they can accomplish things that many experienced practitioners would never have even tried. Regarding this approach to new thinking, the great Buckminster Fuller once said, *"Dare to be naïve."*

My recommendation to you while trying to learn something new here is to take on the attitude that the material being presented is valid, useful to tens of thousands of previous students, and offered to benefit you. If an idea is unfamiliar or upsetting in some way, allow yourself to temporarily suspend your automatic argumentative machinery.

Try the idea on for size and see what happens. If it doesn't immediately make sense, let it percolate for a while to see how it fits into the larger framework of your experiences. Suspend judgment until after you've seen the whole picture. Then, after full consideration, the choice of rejecting or accepting the new idea is up to you. In this way, you will be able to efficiently build the vocabulary of ideas you will need to perceive differently and produce improved leadership results.

How To Begin

If starting to do this work seems daunting, don't be discouraged. Rather, be informed and intentional. Honestly ask and answer the following questions:

• Am I willing and able to tell the truth to myself about where I've been ineffective, deluded, and unaware?

• Am I willing and able to change my mind so I can produce better leadership results?

• Am I willing to take on this self-development project at this time?

If your answer is yes to all the questions above, then you are ready to begin. All you need to do is choose to

28

start. If you choose to proceed, then through mindful and diligent practice, your skill will expand and you will eventually become **unconsciously competent** in the art of leadership.

Think On This

Remember when you were very young and you suddenly realized something new? Many of us can remember the pleasure of *learning* as the learning imprinted in us and became part of our skill set. It was fun.

• In that same spirit of learning, consider what new insights you had while reading this chapter and observing your thoughts, emotions, and body sensations.

New thoughts arise and fall away if not made tangible by writing them down. Other leaders have found that stating an insight in one complete sentence causes a clarity and power that allows the insight to stick with you forever.

• Capture what you learned by writing it down. Begin your insight journal now.

Insights

Insights

Existence and Language

We say the medium of leadership is communication. When you watch a leader in action, he or she is speaking, listening, and demonstrating behavior with his or her body. Leadership is accomplished by connecting with others through communication. Would it be useful to know the effect you have on people and to be able to tune your behavior so that others would understand and act to achieve your intended outcomes? This is the practice in which we'll begin our work. We say that causing a breakthrough in your performance as a communicator will create a breakthrough in your ability to provide effective leadership.

Think back to the time when you gave your first public speech. It might have been in front of a classroom or in a school play or for a music recital. At some point in your history you prepared something like that. Imagine it now. What was it like preparing the presentation in the days before the event? What was it like the day of the event? What were you feeling? What were you thinking? What concerns did you have?

Now imagine what it was like just before walking out onto the stage or up to the front of the room. What was happening in your inner world as you were making that walk? What was it like the first time you put bow to string or sang a melody alone in public? To what were you attending? What did it feel like?

• When you have this experience clearly in mind, write down a few words to capture the thoughts, emotions, and physical sensations you felt.

You experienced a set of emotions, thoughts, visualizations, and body sensations that occurred; you then displayed physical behaviors that could have been videotaped and recorded. All of that was occurring as part of the process of preparing and then performing. After you finished, you walked off stage or back to your seat and then there were the thoughts, emotions, and body sensations that go with self-assessment, something you did immediately after your presentation.

Now ask yourself this question: Where did all those experiences occur? When people confront that question, they typically come up with answers like, "Well, it was happening in my body," or "In my mind," or "It occurred in my feelings." Now ask these questions: *Where* is your mind? Exactly *where* are your feelings? Can you point to them? If we could look into your head, would we see thoughts and emotions? No, we'd see gray matter. We could have videotaped your physical behaviors, but *where* did all that really rich experience of anxiety, thinking, feeling, sensing, creativity, and self-assessment happen?

I have asked that question of thousands of people over the years. Typically, people don't have much to say about it. The question evokes a blank spot in their thinking. We don't have language to answer *where* our inner life occurs. We use the words *mind* or *inner experience* as vague placeholders. Offered below is some language that you can use to clarify your thinking about communication and leadership. It is a basic framework for how human beings experience life. It will aid us in all the rest of the work we do.

The Fields of Existence

There are three experiential realms where things can occur for human beings. These are called **Fields of Existence**.

The first field of existence is the **Foreground**. Everything that appears to be occurring outside the boundary of your skin exists in the Foreground. It is literally present to you and appears to be outside of you. This is a very natural dividing line between events that happen outside of you and ones that happen inside of you in your personal experience.

To understand this, recognize that there is a difference between what appears in your Foreground and what's happening in reality. When you look out into the world, you respond to the things you see there. But have you ever responded to something that you perceived was real and later found out was not? A small child experiences and responds to the imaginary monster he sees under his bed as a real entity in his Foreground. Adults who see and react to monsters that others can't see in their Foreground, are usually thought to be experiencing a psychotic break. What is *actually real* has a measurable physical existence independent of personal interpretation. What *appears to be real* occurs in an individual person's Foreground.

The second field of existence is called the **Midground**. The Midground is your experience of your internal state. The Midground contains all experiences that appear to be occurring inside your body and private space. Midground content includes your body sensations, emotions, thoughts and images that appear to your awareness. You are aware of the contents of your Midground but others are not. As an example, you may have an itch on your left knee but no one appearing in your Foreground will know that, until you physically scratch it or say something about it. They will infer from observing your scratching that you must have an itch but will never directly experience the itch because that body sensation exists only in your personal awareness. The experience is uniquely yours. The experiences of thought, emotion, sensation, and imagination are personal and occur in your Midground.

The third and final field of existence is the **Background**. Your Background contains intentions, beliefs, memories, points of view, biological conditions, etc., all of which are currently unconscious and with which the contents of your Foreground and Midground are consistent. The Background has multiple layers. At the physical level you have body processes like metabolism, inflammation and healing, hormone levels, blood sugar regulation, the polypeptides associated with emotions, other neurotransmitters, your genetic dispositions, and any physical trauma or developmental issues that affect your brain function. At the emotional level of the Background are all our memories of pain and pleasure. At the mental level are stored all your knowledge, beliefs, assumptions, morals, and standards. At the causal and spiritual layers of the Background you have your intentions, purposes, and perennial values.

All of this content runs constantly in the Background and makes up who you are.

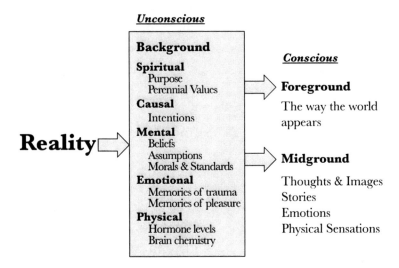

Figure 1: The Fields of Existence

For example, when some people don't eat regularly, their blood sugar level drops and they become irritable. This means that a stimulus experienced directly after a meal might be seen as acceptable, but the same stimulus experienced after not having eaten for four hours might be irritating. The stimulus hasn't changed in reality, but people's perception and reaction to it is different. Why? Because their chemical Background has shifted. The same example applies to hormone levels, the temperament that you were born with, your genetic disposition, the way your brain is wired up with your memory of past fears, past pain, past pleasure, your education, your culture, and your upbringing.

The content of your Background is who you are at any given moment. You are a very rich complex set of programming through which life is experienced as though through colored glasses. As you develop skill, you will be able to choose the filters through which you experience life and be able to detect the filters through which others view it. This awareness of the Background will provide huge advantage in leading people to produce the results you intend to deliver.

A Possible Model for Communication

Most people carry around in their heads a hoped-for model of communication. You have a speaker and you have a listener. If the speaker is skillful, he says exactly what he intends to say into the Foreground. He has a clear intention to communicate something and he actually states it clearly, concisely and cogently. The listener, being a good listener of course, hears exactly what is said and receives the intended communication. How often does that actually happen in real conversation?

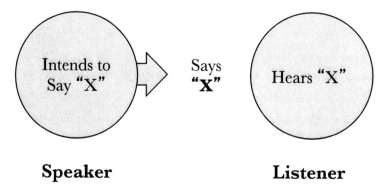

Speaker   **Listener**

Figure 2: The "Hoped For" Model of Communication

There is another possible way of understanding communication that is unlike the conventional model and may prove to be more useful.

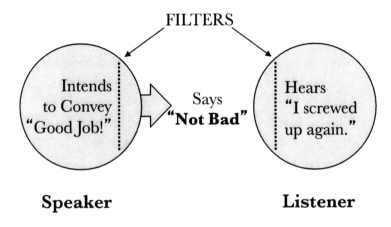

Figure 3: A Possible Model for Communication

Let's give the speaker credit for at least having a clear idea of what he intends to convey. But, because he is a human being, when he does speak he doesn't say exactly what he intends. The speech exists in physical reality as a distorted and somewhat flawed version of what is intended because the information is filtered through a set of criteria in the speaker's Background that shapes what is said. The listener now hears that utterance through the filters of his own Background, further distorting the message. Based on their own experience, most people agree that this model more closely represents what actually happens in real conversations. It's like the first stage of the "telephone" party game where players whisper a phrase into the ear of the person next to them in turn. What each subsequent listener repeats to the next person in line becomes progressively more distorted as the game continues.

As an example, you might be in a business meeting where you are very clear about what you want to say but, when you actually say it, you couch the meaning in words that are politically correct, hoping it will be less dangerous to your career. You layer your speaking with meaning and withhold certain things to make sure it is safe and acceptable. But since we know that people listen through filters in the Background as well, they don't actually hear what you said. *They hear what they say to themselves about what you said.* They hear their interpretation of your interpretation of what you mean. So in fact, you didn't actually say what you wanted to say, and they didn't hear what you actually said or what you intended to say. It's amazing that any understanding occurs between people, given what's on our minds and how we're programmed.

Now you can see that communicating something clearly might require some skill in seeing, hearing, and feeling how the other people are listening so that you can pre-condition your transmission to get through their filters the way that you intend. It is a critically important leadership skill to be able to read someone's mind and then shape your communications so that what is said actually lands the way you'd like it to be taken. This will be our area of concentration. We will be working on understanding how the Background works for human beings so that you can become more skillful at influencing, at inspiring commitment from others, and at having them see and take action on your vision.

Types of Language

Human beings use three types of language as they communicate. You could say that we speak and listen on three different channels simultaneously. The first type of language we use is called **symbolic language**. This is spoken or written language that uses sound symbols to

38

represent particular Midground concepts such as nausea or happiness, or Foreground objects such as automobiles or children. For instance, the word *chair* is the linguistic symbol for a kind of physical object that can support your body while seated in an upright position, without sitting on the ground. The sound *CHe(ə)r* is the auditory symbol that represents that kind of physical object. In other linguistic codes, different symbols represent the same kind of thing. The word *chaise* in French, *silla* in Spanish, and *Stuhl* in German are examples.

E-mail and other written communications exist in symbolic language only. Written language is not particularly good at transmitting emotionally significant communication because it is missing the other two types of human language. Symbolic language, by itself, is useful for little more than data transfer, except in the hands of fine writers who can use symbolic language to create new worlds in the imaginations of creative readers. Prose is an art form that uses symbolic language as its sole medium.

The second type of language that humans use is called **tonal language**. This type uses pitch, timbre, and rhythm to express the kind of communication that occurs on a more primitive level. Your dog, cat, or small child understands tonal language instinctively. Examples of utterances in tonal language include "Mmmmm!" "Wow!" "Whew!" and "Uh-uh!" These sounds do not represent something else. They are themselves the meaning they convey.

The art forms in tonal language are poetry and music, arts that organize sounds and pitches in a way that is beautiful, meaningful and emotionally expressive. You could say that tonal language is the language in which emotion is communicated aurally.

Voice mail contains both symbolic and tonal language. Because it uses two of the three channels available to humans, it is far more effective at carrying the energy, tone, emotion, and drive of a person's communication. It isn't hard to imagine what's on the mind of someone who has left you a voice mail, relative to an e-mail message.

The third and final type of human language is called *gestural language*. This is literally body language and includes thousands of different arrangements of facial muscles, finger and limb positions, postures, and gestures. An art form that uses exclusively gestural language is dance.

More than you can imagine of what we communicate moment to moment is in gestural language. This is why video conferencing and face-to-face meetings are so effective when important decisions must be made. A listener who is fully present in a conversation can achieve a level of rapport with the speaker that borders on psychic connection.

What you say and intone with your mouth may not be true, but your body always expresses the truth in some gestural way. This is why lie detectors work. Poker players train themselves to notice the "tells" of other players so as to detect pretense. The same skill can be applied while leading to detect what is going in the Background. The Background is louder in communication than whatever someone is trying to put into the Foreground.

Think On This

Each day, observe the content of your Midground and write down your insights in this book. What patterns do you see in the flow of thoughts, emotions, and images you experience?

• Notice the impact of tonal and gestural language in your communications with people. Write these insights down.

Insights

Insights

Intention and Attention

In the preceding chapter, we created a language framework that enables us to identify different domains of experience where things occur for human beings. We now have explored the Fields of Existence – Foreground, Midground, and Background. We've considered the idea of filters in the Background through which we view reality. We've named the three different types of language – symbolic, tonal, and gestural, that human beings use to communicate and exercise leadership. In this chapter, we will look at what motivates our actions, what shapes our experiences of our life, and what shapes others' experiences of us.

If you've traveled to a foreign country where you don't know the language, you've likely had the experience of needing to make yourself understood when you were at a linguistic disadvantage. And yet, somehow, you are usually able to connect, get what you need, and be gracious enough to avoid trouble, and at best, make new friends. How is that possible? Since more than half of communication is gestural and a large part is purely tonal, you can see that the majority of your Foreground behavior is not symbolic language. Knowing the language of that country is not absolutely necessary. What you are transmitting is the mood, attitude, point of view, and needs you have in the moment. All of this is intelligible to almost everyone across cultures and language barriers, including young children and animals. With a little creativity, you can add the semantic content required to get what you need through pantomime, gesture, and inference. It's like charades but in service to what you seek.

Intention

Consider this: the driver of that non-verbal communication is your focused *intention* to connect and get what you need. What you intend in the Background shows up in the Foreground. It is well understood by law enforcement officers trained in detecting lies that the body language and galvanic skin response of a subject is a strong indicator for lying, no matter what the person actually says. All it takes for the average person to see this phenomenon in action is to observe someone who is pretending to smile and to notice that their eyes betray the pretense. The fake smile can't move certain muscles around the eyes. Your Background intention always shines through no matter how hard you try. The Background intent is louder than the Foreground pretense. We say that your actual intention in the moment unconsciously drives your behaviors in the Foreground and affects what is transmitted.

Let's clarify exactly what we mean by **intention**. Intention is technically a preemptive brain state that occurs before any action can be taken by humans and complex animals. An intention can be seen in PET scans of a subject's brain about half a second before making a choice or before the muscles move to pick up an object, or before doing any other act of will. A condition arises from the Background just before an action occurs. The subject does not consciously perceive this arising. It shows up later in the Midground as a desire, or, in the Foreground as an observable action. For example, you could desire to take a drink and then extend your arm to bring the drink to your mouth. What you can't know is that before the thought occurred to you, your Background was already in action setting up the conditions in your brain to execute the move.[2] So "who" is driving? Who is the who that's driving you?

We are saying that your intentions are visible to other people and unconsciously influence them even when they are not paying attention. This is why the behaviors of children and animals reflect the unconscious mood and attitude of the people around them. It's why buyers and sellers are so obviously distinct at networking meetings. It's why workers are strongly influenced by a leader's mood, attitude, and state of integrity. The unconscious intentions that are unwittingly communicated into the Foreground cast a shadow over the whole organization, for better or for worse.

This has profound implications for the effectiveness of your leadership. You might agree that being consciously aware of what you truly intend at any given moment would be a useful leadership skill. It would be even more useful if you could shift your intention, in the moment, to produce the result you want with people. This book is about exactly that. To begin to acquire the skill of noticing your intentions, you will need to begin by noticing the effect that your attention has on the people and environment around you.

---

2 Libet, B.; Gleason, C. A.; Wright, E. W.; Pearl, D. K. (1983). "Time of Conscious Intention to Act in Relation to Onset of Cerebral Activity (Readiness-Potential)" Brain 106 (3): 623–42.

Attention

Recall the experience of trying to talk to someone who is not really listening to you. You know the situation well. You're across the meeting table from him trying to communicate something. He is attending to his e-mail or engaged with his hand-held device while you are trying to speak with him or be heard. If you remember an instance like this, you'll recall that it's very hard to speak. You find yourself somewhat tongue-tied. You can barely articulate your thoughts because there's nobody actually receiving what you're trying to transmit. It's extremely frustrating.

Now recall the experience of a conversation where the other person was giving you his full attention. He was really listening to everything about you. He was fully engaged. If you are like most people, it was likely an experience of closeness and connection, a real communing with each other. Your words flowed easily and it was easy to picture what the other person was saying. Your rapport was strong. This is what the word communication really means. It derives from the Latin *comm* (together) *uni* (one) *cation* (the process of...) the process of becoming one together. The author of the *Iliad* and the *Odyssey* gave a classic expression of what is possible in communication:

"Two friends, two bodies with one soul inspired." – Homer, c. 700 B.C.

Attention is where the arrow of your mind is pointed. In communication and in leadership, where you direct your attention is at the core of how you experience others and how others experience you. We say that attention is the essence of experience.

Consider the following example. You are driving down the freeway in the far left lane, doing seventy miles an hour. Three feet from your hip is a cement barrier flying by, and you're not worried at all. Why? Because you're not attending to the median strip. What you're attending to is the music on the radio or the friend you're talking to in the car. Some other part of your brain is operating the car so that you don't run into that median strip. You don't actually experience it. You don't even notice it. If something were written on that median strip, you would not consciously know what it was because your attention is not on it.

Here is another example. Let's say we give you an anesthetic and it renders you unconscious. We then pick you up by your wrists and ankles, bang you into the wall three or four times, sit you down in a chair and then give you the antidote to the anesthetic. When you wake up you would find that, from your point of view, no time had passed; you are bruised and wondering what happened. That whole painful event did not occur for you. It didn't happen in your world because you were not attending to it even though it did happen to your body. When you are in major surgery, your body undergoes all the stress of being operated on but the experience is not present for you consciously. You're not attending to it so it doesn't occur as an experience. No attention or no consciousness yields no present experience.

Intention is the shepherd of *attention*. It is what allows you to point the arrow of your attention. A component part of your Background, your *intentional self*, allows you to direct your attention onto your chosen focus. Some people have an *externally directed* focus of attention. In other words, the instinctive preference of their intentional self is to continually scan the Foreground and Midground for new stimuli and attend to whatever comes up. Other people have a mostly *internally directed* focus of attention. The instinctual preference of these people is to deliberately choose where to direct their attention and to hold it there at will at the expense of all other stimuli. Both preferences have survival value and may be genetic in origin. In either case, the intentional aspect of self directs the attention and by that means determines the content of your experience.

Intention is the force of will; it is your capacity to choose. Assuming you are mentally well, you have the ability to put your attention on whatever you choose. What you attend to gives you the content of your life experience. For example, if most of your attention is persistently on your complaints, what doesn't work about your life, and how unfair your past has been, you will find that your thoughts, emotions, mood, and daily experience will be stressful, unhappy, and unfulfilling. All you need to do to change all that is to put your attention on what is working, what makes you grateful, and the future you are creating. Because what you attend to gives you what you experience, your present will be filled with positive thoughts, emotions, and sensations. With training and practice, you can give up habitually disempowering points of view and adopt ones that allow for a wonderful and satisfying experience of life. With practice, it's also possible for you to lead others to do the same.

Leadership, Intention, and Desire

We say that to lead others effectively you first have to master and develop your own intentional self. To align and direct the intentionality of others, you need to manage your self so that your words, your actions, and your experience of the world are consistent with producing the results you want to achieve with and through people. Having a weak intentional self and little ability to self-manage makes you vulnerable to the vagaries of your animal reactions. When you are competent in this discipline, you are able to lead effectively in the face of resistance, argument, and difficult circumstances. You will be able to cause your attention to go where it will make a difference, not to where your animal reactive self would direct it.

For example, you may have the intention to have a wonderful intimate marriage with your spouse for the rest of your life. As you travel through life, you may happen to meet other people along the way who would make very interesting partners for a variety of compelling reasons. You experience a strong Midground *desire* to engage with those people, but you know that doing so comes at some risk. You can attend to the Midground experience of desire, or you can intentionally put your attention on your standing commitment to your marriage. You get to choose between being driven by your desires and honoring your committed purpose in the Background. This ability to choose one's actions in the presence of internal conflict is a source of power for human beings and what is meant by self-management and the practice of integrity. We will explore this capacity more fully in Chapter 9.

The same kinds of situations happen in practical leadership. You always face the choice between doing what you desire to be comfortable and safe, and doing what would serve the purpose you are fulfilling as a leader. In your leadership role, will you attend to your appetites, your feelings, and how exhausted you are, or will you attend to your intention to make a difference for your people? If you are consciously intentional, you will have many possible choices.

One of the most effective ways to build the power of the intentional self is meditation. Entry-level meditation, no matter what technique you are using, is the practice of directing your wandering attention back to the anchor of the meditation – a repeating Midground thought, sound, or image, or a Foreground object of attention. It's the practice of training your intentional self to focus your attention where you want it to be. In the beginning of your training, Meditation 1.0 is the practice of noticing where your attention goes automatically and then shifting it back to where you want it to be. This is building the muscle of intentionality that is required for effective leadership. Once you can reliably direct and hold your attention through clear intentionality, you can begin to practice Meditation 2.0 where you create other more blissful experiences like being in the timeless presence of delight, wonder, and awe. Many advanced levels of attainment can be achieved by experienced practitioners.

Many experts in the area of learning and development say that meditation is the fastest way to enhance your ability to think and to perceive. It is also the most efficient way to advance the complexity and intentionality of your consciousness. It is possible to develop more in three year's time than most non-practitioners will develop in their whole lifetime. Meditation also has many other salutary effects in that it reorganizes your Background. It enables higher levels of emotional resilience, lower levels of stress and internal noise. You acquire an enhanced ability to see things from many different points of view. You could say that the practice is a sure pathway to gaining wisdom and courage in the face of difficulty. It's also a very pleasant daily practice for busy leaders.

Meditation is highly recommended for people who are expanding their capacities to lead effectively. Find a teacher and a method that is compatible with your culture, personality, and personal value system. When you have gone as far as you can go with that technique as measured by your ability to focus your attention powerfully, move on to the next, more demanding approach. Using meditation to grow and develop is not so much about being right as it is about being able to intend and to create.

Think On This

Observe where your attention goes. What do you habitually attend to?

How often do you do what makes you comfortable, at the expense of being an effective leader? If it's more often than you know is good for you and your people, begin to pay attention to making the future great and less attention to making yourself comfortable.

• Meditation works. If you are not meditating as a daily practice now, why not? If you wish to begin, inquire into the many different practices available to see what fits you best. Then start your own practice.

• Record the insights you generated from inquiring into the topics above in your insight journal.

★

Insights

Parasitic Memory Activation

We just examined how our intention is the shepherd of our attention. We have the ability to choose what we attend to and, if we are skilled and awake, what drives our actions. But often in life, reactions come up from the Background that completely rob us of any conscious choice in the matter of our experiences and our behaviors. These reactions are intense automatic responses that tend to overcome us and use all our channels for their own ends. You're used by some mechanism that pops up out of the Background and takes you over. It's you at your worst. You can't be an effective leader when you're having a reaction like this. This chapter provides a way to take yourself back and return yourself to being effective when the Background has taken over.

Here is an example. One day I was driving from Sonoma County down to Oakland for a meeting. I hadn't driven to Oakland in many months. As I approached the Interstate 80/580 interchange, I realized that I was in a construction zone. The situation looked very different than I remembered. When I tried to merge onto 580, I couldn't see how to do it, and I took what looked like an off-ramp that I thought was going to curve around to 580. In fact, it was the on-ramp to the Bay Bridge, and to make matters worse, it was the lane that only buses are supposed to use.

But there was no way for me to know I was in the wrong lane until I was all the way around the curve.

As soon as I rounded the curve, a California Highway Patrolman was standing there with a really aggresive look on his face pointing at me shouting, "Stop the car!" He made commanding gestures to make me pull over and stop. He was on foot so he could ticket every driver that came through the turn. What a setup!

The moment I saw him give me the "Pull over!" command, something took me over. It was an instantaneous adrenaline rush. There was a metallic taste in my mouth. My heart started to beat faster. My thoughts were filled with language like, "Oh @&#%^$!" I experienced a mix of strong negative emotions. I pulled to the side of the roadway and began to look for my license and registration. I was so upset that I couldn't even find my wallet. I looked everywhere but I couldn't see the it.

The officer came up to the window and said, "License and registration," in a really gruff tone of voice. I said, "I'm sorry, I'm looking." He could see that my wallet was actually on my lap but that I was trying to find it in the glove box.

When he pointed this out to me, I became more aware of the Foreground. I began to settle down. I was able to give him the license and registration. He saw that I was from a little town in Sonoma County and believed me when I said that I didn't know where I was going. Because he saw that I was sincerely upset by the situation, he generously gave me the instructions on how to get to where I wanted to go and let me proceed without issuing a ticket.

54

As I pulled away, I again got to marvel at how powerful my Background is when it takes me over and incapacitates me. This is an example of what we're going to call *Parasitic Memory Activation* or PMA.

It's parasitic because, when it activates, it actually robs you of your capacities and your mental bandwidth. It is a memory activation because something happens in the Foreground or Midground that triggers a takeover of your functions by your Background machinery. The example I described above was a very intense PMA that affected me for hours afterwards. It's also possible to have very subtle ones.

For instance, I used to travel about 24 weeks per year doing consulting and training all over the world for an East Coast-based consulting firm. The agreement that we had as consultants with the home office in Connecticut was that we would check our voicemail every 24 hours, no matter where we were, so that we would be in contact and reachable.

One day, I was waiting at some airport in Europe dialing into my voicemail as agreed. The system announced that I had six messages and began to play through them. Before each message, the name of the person leaving the message was played. At the beginning of message four, the system said, "Message from Rudy Stahl." Rudy Stahl was my boss, the Director of Education. Rudy almost never called me except when he wanted something or when something was wrong. When I heard that voice tag and that particular tone of voice, "Rudy Stahl", something inside me sank. It was like, *"Oh @&#%^$!!"* accompanied by negative emotions in the fear category. At that moment, what I looked like in the Foreground was simply a person holding the phone with a blank expression on his face. But what was occurring in my Midground was an automatic reaction. The memories of my experiences and conversations with Rudy were all brought into the present. In that moment, as soon as I heard that stimulus, those trigger words on that voicemail tag, I was in a Parasitic Memory Activation.

Why are we talking about this? Because as leaders, things happen all the time that cause PMAs and we need to be able to recover our full functionality and ourselves as soon as possible. If you are speaking in front of a group of people making a presentation and someone raises his or her hand and asks a question that triggers you, you'd better be able to recover yourself and get back in the game in a few seconds or the likelihood of your success will be very diminished.

Similarly, when you are at a meeting and someone says something upsetting to you, and you don't then say what you want to in return (because it would be politically dangerous or unprofessional) that can cause a PMA. You think about the situation for the next 24 hours mulling it over and over in your mind. You're on the pillow that night saying to yourself, "If I had only said ..." You're rehearsing or reviewing and wishing it had gone differently. It's just grinding you and you can't let it go. That's a PMA. When a PMA is in progress, you can't leave the problem at work and then be with the people at home because you're grinding on what some person said to you at a meeting. That's called Parasitic Memory Activation.

So to review, when you're in a PMA, there is no conscious intentionality. It's as though there is a part of you that is using most of your bandwidth and it won't let you go. You can't move on. As long as it has a grip on you, you remain less than your normal effective self. This is what distinguishes a PMA from any other reaction – you are incapacitated and have no choice in the matter.

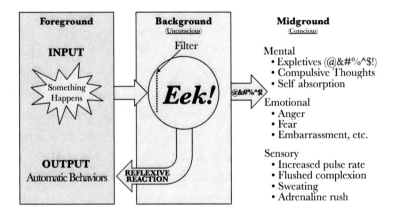

Figure 4: Parasitic Memory Activation

PMAs are mechanisms that have a particular config-uration. In the beginning, something happens in the Fore-ground that triggers the event. The sensory experience of this stimulus is processed through the Background, as usu-al, but in the case of a PMA, the processing causes am-plification and distortion. The stimulus activates memories of past physical, emotional, and mental pain stored in the Background. The emotional impact of those memories are summed together and hooked to the simple experience of the triggering event. Your body responds with automatic be-havior in the Foreground and compulsive thoughts, negative emotions, and stressful body sensations in the Midground. There is no thinking or choosing going on – only automatic reactions and uncomfortable feelings and thoughts.

57

Unhooking Yourself from a PMA

It is possible to develop a skill of self-management that allows for immediately extinguishing a PMA as soon as it begins. Shown below is a tried and true method to deal with a PMA.

1 – Notice the PMA

First notice that you have been triggered and that a PMA has you in its grip. As soon as you do this, you will have differentiated yourself from the reaction. The PMA will not have you – you will have it. After you get skilled at taking PMAs apart, you may only need to do this one first step to free yourself. But if, after recognizing you've been triggered and the PMA is still active, proceed to Step 2.

2 – Identify the stimulus

Just a minute ago, you were fine. Then something happened and you found yourself in the PMA. Exactly what happened that lit you up like a war zone? It will always be something you sensed in the Foreground or a thought you had in the Midground.

3 – Classify the stimulus

It turns out that anything can be a PMA stimulus. You go into a kitchen, see stacked dishes in the sink and are triggered. You could go into your bedroom, see some socks on the floor and be triggered. You could see a flashing red light in your rear view mirror and be triggered.

The trigger itself is often trivial. From an external point of view, "socks on the floor" may only be socks on the floor.

But because of the particular Background of memories, standards, beliefs, and ideologies you have, "socks on the floor" connects to a whole series of memories that, taken together, have a huge emotional impact. All those memories get brought into the present because they're incidents that are linked in your mind. The collective weight of all those experiences occurs in the Now. This is why the reaction seems so out of proportion to the stimulus.

PMA stimuli fall into four categories:

1) ***Reminders of pain or fear*** – e.g., Going back to a place that reminds you of a painful time in the past can bring up negative emotions and uncomfortable body sensations that are hard to shake.

2) ***Unwanted surprises or obstacles*** – e.g., The CHP officer was an example of an unwanted surprise. An example of an unwanted obstacle is not being able to print an important document you need just before a meeting.

3) ***Reminders of breaches of integrity*** – e.g., You run into someone at work that you gossiped about. In the past, you damaged the person's reputation with a third party even though you knew that gossiping is wrong. Running into the subject of the gossip reminds you of the breach of your own integrity with all the negative emotions and thoughts that go with it.

4) ***Violations of your standards or ideals*** – e.g., Seeing unwashed dishes stacked in the sink is a great example. Seeing or hearing anything that isn't "the way it should be" can be a PMA stimulus.

4 – Choose to be responsible

If you haven't gotten past the PMA by that point, you can ask yourself, "Am I willing to be responsible for my own programming?" You could realize that the stimulus, taken by itself, is usually trivial. The intensity of the reaction often isn't proportional to the stimulus. It's a function of your own memories. You could see that you make yourself upset about what is triggering you.

5 – Choose to remain in the PMA or let it go

Ask yourself, "Am I willing to be responsible for my own programming?" If the answer is no, that's fine. You can have the PMA for as long as you wish. It's your life. If the answer is yes, "I take responsibility for my own programming," then you can choose NOT to be upset. I recommend that you choose to be responsible and return to being happy and effective.

"In life, pain is inevitable. Suffering is optional." – Haruki Murakami, *What I Talk About When I Talk About Running*

How to help others with PMAs

As you begin to practice these five steps, you may feel like you are having more PMAs, at first. By putting your attention on your automatic reactions, they will be more present in your experience. Actually, they were happening all the time; you just thought they were normal. Until you wake up, you live a highly reactive life. As you continue to practice unhooking yourself, PMAs will lose their power over you. After more practice in taking PMAs apart, the number of stimuli will decrease.

There's a lot of programming in the Background. The older you get, the more there is. If we're interested in self-development and becoming effective leaders, we benefit from mastering our PMAs, and practicing unhooking so often that we eventually become impreturbable.

There is something *that happens in the world* and there is something *that happens in your head.* Can you be responsible for what happened in your head? Yes, you can. And, if you are, you can make intentional choices to cause things to happen in reality. That's called leadership – causing things to happen out in the world that move the group, yourself, or the situation, in the direction that is of service to the group you're leading.

People catch PMAs from other people who are having PMAs. People who are reacting cause other people in their surroundings to react. It's almost like a magnetic field that others get sucked into. The ability to willfully observe what's happening in the Foreground and distinguish it from your internal reactions is the key skill. It's one of the fundamental skills of self-development and leadership.

As leaders and managers, we intend to be sensitive to people's programming so as to not cause upset. But it's impossibly complex to take everyone's unique programming into account before you speak. What is possible, once you learn this method yourself, is to help people notice that they're having a PMA and to help them out of it.

Instead of saying, "Why are you upset?" you can say, "What happened? What caused the reaction?" Asking, "What happened?" directs their attention from their Midground experience to Foreground reality. Putting their attention on reality enables them to disassociate from the automaticity of the reaction. It's really just the skill of using their intention to direct their attention. You can help people do that. As you listen to "what happened," you can help them discern the PMA stimulus and its classification. Usually, if you provide an unbiased way of listening, they will eventually unhook themselves and stop suffering.

Think On This

As you begin to observe PMAs, you will notice that there seem to be more and more of them in your life. Consider that they were there all the time and instead of resolving them, you probably just tolerated them until you could "get over it." Practice unhooking yourself daily. Eventually you can become imperturbable.

• Write down the stimuli for your PMAs and in what classification they are. (reminders of pain or fear, unwanted surprises or obstacles, reminders of breeches of integrity, violations of standards or ideals)

• What insights arise from your newfound awareness?

Insights

Insights

Introduction to
the Modes of Intention

Let's take a moment to reflect upon what we've learned so far. We've seen that the programming running in the Background through which we view the world profoundly influences our subjective reality. It filters all the sensory data that we absorb and selectively presents information to our consciousness, based on a currently unconscious set of criteria determined by the sum total of the experiences in our memory and our current physical state. The Background filtering at the biological, chemical, emotional, and intellectual levels of ourselves profoundly shapes what we see in the world and what it means to us. In a very real way, the way the world looks to us is only a reflection of ourselves.

"We don't see things as they are, we see them as we are." – Anaïs Nin

We've seen that the intention we have in the Background drives our thinking and therefore our behaviors, especially in the way we speak and listen. Another way to say this is that the Background and what appears to be in the Foreground are always correlated. If the socks on the floor cause a parasitic memory activation (PMA) in you, how the socks appear in the Foreground and your

Midground experience of negative emotions, compulsive thoughts, and stress symptoms are completely correlated to your Background programming. It's not just "socks on the floor" or "lights left on." For you, it's a betrayal, or evidence of defiance, or something more "important" to you. Even while reacting, you may notice that your behavior is out of proportion to the stimulus. You experience having no choice in the matter and feel as though you are held hostage, disempowered by random events with a diminished ability to lead.

We've also seen that it's possible to shift your intention in the Background to serve your purpose by the application of your will. You can actually unhook yourself. You can regain self-control when you're set on autopilot by disengaging the PMA. It's one of the ways that we can demonstrate our true humanity instead of remaining unconsciously reactive. Human beings have the capacity to shift their attention and modify their intentions in any circumstance. We have a choice, if we exercise that choice. We can free ourselves from the boundaries of constrained reflexive behaviors and their unintended negative consequences.

In the next chapters, we will focus on how our Background intentions shape the way we speak and listen, and how that impacts our ability to produce results with and through other people. Why this approach? Because knowing what is really driving your behavior and the way you see the world enables you to be more effective with yourself, and by extension, with other people. As individual as we are, human beings share a universal operating system. Knowing how that system works will give you the keys to leadership, creativity, and power.

As a possible way to think about the human operating system, we offer a framework of interpretation called "*The Modes of Intention*."

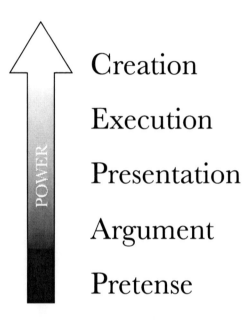

Creation

Execution

Presentation

Argument

Pretense

Figure 5: The Five Modes of Intention

Each mode drives a particular way of speaking, listening, behaving, and experiencing the world. There are only five modes. The Modes of Intention are similar to radio buttons in your car. You can only be in one intentional mode at a given time.

The next three chapters will reveal the Modes of Intention that suppress leadership, creativity, and power. After they are fully explored, and their effects made clear, the source of power for human beings is discussed and the Modes that are the foundation for effective leadership and accomplishment will be distinguished. The first mode we will consider is the *Mode of Presentation*.

Insights

The Mode of Presentation

Imagine that you're sitting in a theater-style conference session with hundreds of people. The lights go down and a presenter appears at the podium. He is wearing a microphone and his PowerPoint deck is on the screen. He begins talking and changing slides. After about five minutes, what starts to happen in your Midground experience? You initially were thinking thoughts about the presenter, the presentation, its relevance to you, your level of agreement with the content, and so on. As the show continues, you may actually find yourself thinking about something entirely different, trying to escape the increasing levels of boredom. After about another five minutes, you may begin thinking to yourself, "When is this going to end?" And in yet another five minutes (in which time has flowed very slowly) you may actually be nodding off to sleep. We call that experience "Death by Power Point."

It's a common experience. It's why when you present, the audience may ask you for the slides after you've given your presentation. It may be because they haven't really been listening. They're more focused on their opinion of what you're saying and internally commenting on it. In the Mode of Presentation, people don't listen to what you actually say. They hear what they say to themselves about what you said. After about ten minutes, they just can't listen to you anymore. This is a phenomenon we're going to call *listening* in the Mode of Presentation.

From the speaker's point of view, what is it like to prepare your presentation? On what are you focused? You're focused on:

"Will I look good?"

"Does this look cool enough?"

"Did I use the right language to get it across?"

"Are there too many words on the slide?"

"What should I wear?"

"What's going to work best?"

As you approach the podium and begin doing your presentation, you begin assessing yourself while presenting. What are you concerned about? You're concerned about:

"Do they like me?

"Do they accept me?

"Is this working?

"If someone interrupts me with a question that makes me have to jump to slide 58, when I'm only at slide 26, what then?"

This has now become a PMA trigger (an unwanted obstacle) because it's completely off-purpose from what you want to accomplish. Does this sound familiar? This is the experience of *speaking* in The Mode of Presentation.

What insights can we glean from this? The majority of business conversations occur in the Mode of Presentation. If you record eight hours of video in a meeting room of any corporation you will likely see that over four hours of the dialog is about transferring information and expressing opinions. Is it necessary? It's completely necessary. You've got to transfer information in business. People need to express their opinions and make recommendations, give analyses, and provide reports. The problem with this kind of speaking and listening is that it drives people unconscious and then they ask you for the slides which they then may or may not look at. If you look carefully, you'll see that presentations seldom cause action in and of themselves. They just provoke more opining, analyses, and consideration and cause people to go to sleep or distract themselves with mobile devices.

Why? Consider this question, "Whose opinion is the most important opinion in the world?" Mine! My opinion, of course. Guess what? That's true for everybody else on the planet as well. How long can people actually tolerate listening to *your* opinion? It turns out to be not very long. People can take about five to seven minutes of pure presentation. Once you've passed the five-minute mark, their buffers are getting full. When you're at seven minutes, people start glazing over and start thinking about something else. Why? Because people cannot tolerate listening to somebody else's point of view for that long without expressing *what they want to say about what was said*. People need to outflow every five to seven minutes to dump their buffer. When the buffer is empty, they can then listen to the next segment to be presented.

In the Mode of Presentation, your Background intent is to share information from your point of view and to be understood, admired, and accepted by others. While speaking in this mode, the focus of your attention is absorbed with "getting it right." You want to come across as smart and compelling. You need your audience to buy into what you are presenting. This drive (and need) is the source of all of the fear that people experience when they prepare and deliver presentations. It's a fundamental human need to belong and to be admired by the others.

As a *listener* in the Mode of Presentation, your focus of attention is on listening for understanding and relevance. If you find that a presentation is irrelevant to you, you are going to disconnect and handle your e-mail or text messages instead. While listening, you filter for points of personal value and interest as in, "What's useful to me? All the rest of it I'm discarding and into the mental shredder it goes." You just want to know what's in it, for you.

The Mode of Presentation has advantages and disadvantages. The advantages are that it transfers data to others about you and your opinions. The disadvantages are that it produces no action and can stupefy your audience. You can transfer information all you want, all day long, but if that is all that happens, no committed action will result. It will produce more of the content of the mode itself – opinions, justifications, explanations, rationalizations, reports on what I think, etc.

The Midground content in this mode at the mental level is assessments and judgments on what's being presented, e.g. "I like it/I don't like it. I agree/I disagree. It's relevant/It's not relevant." At the emotional level, we

experience increasing boredom and irritation. At the phys-
ical-sensory level, we experience a decreasing awareness of
the Foreground, a dilated sense of time; we might even fall
asleep. Five minutes can seem like twenty.

The Foreground behavior in this mode includes opinions, explanations, analyses, rationalizations, reports,
descriptions, sharing of emotional states as in emotional
weather reports about how I feel, how my day went, the
details of an emotional conversation, etc. In the Mode of
Presentation it's all about my opinion and me. It's ego on
loudspeaker.

Think On This

It is thought that up to eighty per cent (80%) of
conventional business communication is in the Mode of
Presentation. This is a tremendous challenge, especially if
you intend to lead a group into dynamic and committed
action. In business, you've got to transfer data. How do you
use this modality in a way that's actually valuable to your
audience so that they engage with you?

 • Less is more. Every word counts. Do not repeat yourself. People have limited attention spans. Be efficient
 and clear. Cut out verbal and visual deadwood.

 • Speak in service to your audience or those you lead,
 not yourself. This is not about you. If you make the presentation for them, they will think it's relevant. They
 will listen to you. Why? Because it's about what they
 care about. In the Mode of Presentation, where the ego
 is on loudspeaker, it's usually all about "Me!" Instead,
 say only what they would find useful.

• Work on being interested, not interesting. Have your presentation be about, "What are these people interested in hearing? What's relevant to them? What can I give them that would be of service to them?"

The Mode of Presentation is the norm. What are the alternatives? How can you use this information to improve your communications?

• Write these insights down.

Insights

Insights

The Mode of Argument

In the previous chapter, we saw that underlying the Mode of Presentation is a Background intention to share information about your point of view and to be understood, admired, and accepted by others. This intentional mode produces a particular set of filters for speaking, listening, and viewing the world that focuses our attention on our own interests and ourselves, with a similar shift to self-absorption in the audience.

Consider this question: what is it like to speak, listen, and view the world when your point of view changes from, "The way I see things is my opinion" to "The way I see things is The Truth"? What is it like to be in a conversation where some or all of the parties take the stance that their way of seeing things is actually and uniquely "The way it is" or "The way it should be," and there is no other option? ("My way or the highway.")

In this chapter, we examine the *Mode of Argument*. In this mode, your Background intention is to maintain and promote your strongly held point of view as "The Truth." Your speaking and listening in this mode has an automatic impact on people. To get a feel for this, remember that theater-style conference session from last chapter? This time be a member of the audience. You're sitting with hundreds of people. The lights go down and a presenter appears at the podium. He is wearing a microphone and his PowerPoint deck is on the screen. He begins talking and the first thing he says is, "Business people always make better managers than engineers."

Stop and listen to what you are saying to yourself. What is the first thought that popped into your Midground the instant you read, "Business people always make better managers than engineers."?

If you are like most people, the first automatic reaction to that statement is an argument either for or against. When I demonstrate this effect in trainings, people experience an automatic Midground response like "Damn right!" or "Wait a second!" In a fraction of a second, the Background offers up a yes or no response. People are taking sides before they even are aware of it. At that moment, an argument begins. Communications in the Mode of Argument beget more argument.

As with all the Modes of Intention, when you speak in this mode, you automatically trigger your audience to listen in this mode.

Let's look at another example: consider political attack ads. By stating a negative message as though it is fact, the audience polarizes around the idea. If people already agree, their point of view gets re-energized and confirmed. They experience increased validation for their point of view. If people disagree, they automatically argue, "That's wrong!" as soon as they see the ad and become more adversarial in their point of view. Almost no one's opinions actually change. That's okay, because the primary effect of attack ads is to mobilize the base, not change opinions.

The net outcome is that people are riled up and even more wedded to their positions.

When in the Mode of Argument, people are at work trying to convince one another that their point of view is right. The word "convince" comes from the Latin *convincere* (to overcome), *con-* being the prefix meaning "with" and *vincere* meaning "to conquer." So, if you are at work trying to convince someone of something, you are trying to vanquish him or her through winning an argument. This stance automatically calls forth the same defensive mode of intention from your opponent. In this war-like scenario, trying to convince someone that you are right requires that they concede they are wrong. Someone has to capitulate, suffer humiliation, and defeat for the other to prevail. Very few egos are capable of accepting this as good thing, which makes winning arguments an uphill battle. People really hate to be wrong.

Even though it's neither a skillful nor effective way to accomplish things, taking the tack of trying to convince people is typical in work cultures. Sales people, who try to motivate their customers to act by convincing them, instead of inspiring committed action, know how hard life is in the Mode of Argument. One could say that science is a 500 year long argument in which new theories arise and are pounded to dust by competing ideas and competing egos. The ideas that survive the rigors of scientific examination become the current state of the art. In high tech businesses, for example, analytical engineering cultures and their problem/solution-based orientation are all grounded in argument. Experience shows that truly innovative collaboration is almost impossible in this kind of environment.

Think back to a workday where, from the moment you arrive at your desk, your attention is preoccupied with what's not working, what's broken, the problems you have to solve and how people could actually make something happen, if they would just get their act together. Circumstances don't go your way. Everything seems to be hard. The meetings you attend are filled with people making their case, gossiping, complaining, and trying to get their ways. Does this sound familiar? If you can place yourself in a day like that, you will recall the feeling of an environment driven by argument.

In the Mode of Argument, your Background intention is to maintain and promote your strongly held point of view, as "The Truth." You speak to convince others that you are right and that something or someone is wrong. When listening, the focus of your attention is on collecting evidence and gaining agreement from others to bolster your strongly held point of view. You are assessing, "Is that in agreement with my truth or not?" The thinking is black and white. If they agree with you, you feel gratified and supported. If not, before they are even done talking, you are already thinking about what you're going to say to change their minds.

There are benefits to operating in this intentional mode. It can be used to motivate action and bolster support with those who already agree with you. The costs that come with those benefits are creating a negative polarized environment, provoking even more argument, sapping your energy, and increasing stress for everyone. The more you use Mode of Argument speaking and listening, the greater and more widespread the negative effects become.

In the mental domain of the Midground, the thinking is binary, judgmental, reactive, and righteous. In the emotional domain, you experience anger, frustration, glee at the downfall of others, and depression. At the sensory level, you experience exaggerated stress symptoms, dilated time, and increasing levels of drowsiness. It takes a lot of life energy to maintain and defend the rightness of a strongly held point of view against all others.

Foreground speaking in the Mode of Argument includes arguments of any kind, complaints, gossip, insults, sarcasm, slurs, and other speech the context of which is, "I'm right about this and you are wrong if you disagree with me." Living habitually in this mode makes the world look like there is always something wrong, something to be fixed, a problem to solve, or some circumstance or relationship where you are the guiltless party, and the circumstances are running the show. Unfortunately, it seems that most people are in the Mode of Argument most of the time.

> NOTE: At this point in the chapter, you may find yourself having an argument with this text. If that is the case, examine the strongly held point of view in which you are embedded and how automatically your Background is trying to prove your case. Remember that there is no one here to convince. You are reading a book.

Complaints

"I personally think we developed language because of our deep inner need to complain." – Jane Wagner

Complaints are the primary verbal behavior of someone embedded in the Mode of Argument. A complaint is a Foreground statement or a Midground thought that something is unacceptable or unsatisfactory. Clearly, if something or someone is wrong, you are very right about that, and you are holding forth promoting your strongly held point of view as "The Truth" only to suffer the negative social and psychological effects that go with it.

Complaints come in four varieties. The first is a *recreational* complaint. This is the kind of complaint people use to connect with each other or to promote themselves with others. "Can you believe the 49ers game yesterday? They were robbed!" or, "I can't believe they paired chardonnay with this dish. Seriously?" Both complaints are designed to show off a particular expertise or tribal status and are applied in a conversation to engage someone in social interaction. Recreational complaints can also include personal weather reports such as, "I am just exhausted!" or any other complaint that is designed to engage a listener, lubricate the conversation, or fill uncomfortable silences.

The second type of complaint is a *therapeutic* complaint. The intention of this complaint is to clear a negative emotional state by sharing the complaint with another person. We say that we need "to get something off our chest." If the complaint is delivered and is fully heard without resistance, it disappears. This is how you know it is a therapeutic complaint. The listener's job is to hold the bucket for the other person. When they are done, they will actually be done with the complaint. Some people make the mistake of trying to fix the complaint, while it is being delivered. This only makes matters worse because the complainer is trying to clear the negative emotion, not fix the problem. The downside of therapeutic complaints is that they involve at least one other person and maybe others in the negative effects of the Mode of Argument. The repercussions can be unwanted and even career limiting. As an example, consider the effect on your career of using your boss or a customer as the bucket holder for your therapeutic complaint. If not done responsibly, the damage to your reputation may be irritating at best and irreparable at worst.

The third type of complaint is called a **persistent** complaint. A persistent complaint is one that you keep repeating over a long period of time, but no matter what you say or what you do it keeps coming back as an active unresolved issue in your life. These are the most pernicious type of complaints because the strongly held point of view that powers them is so fixed in your Background that it shapes your view of reality. It actually seems that you have no power to influence the situation no matter what you do. The stories that comprise persistent complaints always cast you in the role of the guiltless party trying your best and the other parties or circumstances are beyond your control. We will address this toxic point of view in Chapter Eight and offer an antidote.

Finally, there is a fourth kind of complaint that we'll label as a **committed** complaint. A committed complaint is one that you deliver as a prelude to causing an action to resolve the issue you are complaining about. When children want something, sometimes they will state their request in the form of a committed complaint. When children whine, "I'm hungry!" it is an immature request for something to eat. "It's too cold in here!" said in a complaining tone is a manipulative way to get someone to turn up the heat. The equivalent in a business context could be "I don't have enough budget!" which is an irresponsible way of asking for more money to spend. "Frank has got to go!" is a melodramatic way of requesting that Frank be removed from the project team. Committed complaints are the best of type of complaints, but they are still the least skillful way to move action forward and they carry all the ill effects consistent with the Mode of Argument.

Gossip

Another kind of speech in the Mode of Argument is *gossip*. Gossip means idly conversing about a person in a way you would not do, if the subject of the gossip were present. Gossip of any kind is in the Mode of Argument because the gossiper has a strongly held point of view about another person, is going about promoting that point of view, and is gathering evidence and agreement that it is correct.

To be clear, conversing privately about a person in the context of personnel management or training and development is not gossip because it is not idle conversation. The purpose of the conversation is to manage a business resource or develop a person's knowledge, skills, and abilities. It does not damage the trust, respect, integrity, or performance of the participants or the subject of the conversation.

There is a particularly dangerous kind of gossip that can sink careers, kill employee morale, and create an environment of fear, uncertainty and distrust in its wake. Also known as *calumny*, malicious gossip is conversation containing false statements that are intended to damage the reputation, the ability to work, or the credibility of another person. It's closely related to slander. Slander is a civil wrong or tort that can be the basis for a lawsuit. Malicious

84

gossip erodes trust, respect, and is considered by many human resources experts to be an *ad hominem* attack and a form of workplace violence.

As with complaining, many people seem almost compelled to gossip. There is a psychological benefit that gossipers get from promoting their points of view, getting a false sense of power, and being the source of sensational information in their social group. But along with those benefits come costs. Gossipers and complainers are seen by others as people who are not to be trusted. People think, If I share information with the gossiper, it might be used against me. Hurt feelings, damaged reputations, and people taking sides in an "us versus them" scenario are created. Productivity is lost, and time is wasted. Gossip and complaining are erosive of trust and the morale of a group. And yet, it seems that there is a never-ending fountain of complaints and gossip whenever human beings work together in groups unless someone has led the team out of that quagmire.

The Group Effects of Argument

People that work in environments where the Mode of Argument is prevalent suffer certain negative psychological and physiological effects. An environment filled with complaints, gossip, negative assessments, and arguments sucks the life out of people. With so many people involved in the negative discourse, it seems like there is no hope for the future. It's almost impossible to be effective, creative, and innovative in this space. Individuals begin to talk to themselves, complaining internally about the complainers and how negative the place is; they contribute to the energy of Argument. When people articulate their complaints about the complaining and gossip, it snowballs, and others are included in the contagion of depression. More sick days are taken, greater attrition of high value resources occurs, and a mood of conflict and suppression builds. The energy in the Mode of Argument spirals down and out, increasing in size with the mass of the conversation. Is it any wonder that people go home exhausted at night? If they live with others, they may arrive at home and find another environment of complaints and arguments. It seems that the default mode for human beings is the Mode of Argument.

Consider that your Background is in this mode almost all of the time. It's instinctual. Some people have called this phenomenon the Inner Critic. Something is always wrong about you, about them, about the situation, about the world. When you give voice to those Midground thoughts, you include others in your persistently negative point of view.

Consider that as a leader of a group it is fundamentally counterproductive to speak and listen in the Mode of Argument. The costs are too high for you personally and too high for the group you lead. It's the quickest way to suck the life out of your team and to undermine your ability to cause positive change. If you need to complain, do it responsibly with a peer who is willing to hold the bucket for you. Never complain or criticize within earshot of your team. They will repeat your negative assessments throughout the gossip network and your disheartening words will bring the whole group down. This is especially true for leaders, because their complaints are more credible and carry more weight than the complaints of the rank and file.

Think On This

Do you see that you have indulged in the Mode of Argument at work? What do you now see the cost of that has been to you and your team?

How does speaking and listening in this way affect your life at home and in your community?

Insights

Insights

The Mode of Pretense

In this chapter, we will consider how people try to get what they want when they feel unsafe and are unable to change the circumstances or exercise their personal power.

Scenario: You and your spouse are invited to your manager's house for dinner. As you pull up to their house and park the car, your sweetheart pulls down the mirror on the sunshade and checks for anything out of place. You ask, "Okay. What's the signal for the time to leave?"

She says, "The usual. What are their names again?"

"Bob and Denise" you answer. "Remember to compliment the kitchen remodel. They're really proud of that. And their kids are named Johnny and Sara."

As she finishes the final adjustments, she says, "You owe me one for this... Okay, let's do this thing."

As you approach the front door and ring the doorbell, she asks, "How do I look?"

Before you can answer, Denise opens the door and declares in an overly happy voice, "Oh it's SO great to see you!" to which you both respond, "Finally! It's been SO long!" as though you were reuniting with a long lost family member.

Scenario: You are in a meeting at work. One of the participants is someone who you find irritating and with whom you find it difficult to communicate. He says something argumentative and it triggers a strong reaction in you. You strongly disagree with what he said, but because he is senior to you and it is politically dangerous to challenge him directly you say, "Help me understand how you came to that conclusion." Later that day, you pass him in the hall and say, "Hey, John! That was a great meeting this morning."

Scenario: A colleague of yours is giving a music recital. It's taken him six months to prepare the repertoire, but preparation notwithstanding, his performance is quirky, idiosyncratic, and unconvincing. Because you are colleagues, you are obliged to go backstage afterwards and congratulate him. As you come to the front of the line you shake his hand, look him in the eye, and say, "That was really something! I've never heard anything like it. The Brahms is such a beautiful piece. Truly amazing!"

These are three examples of people operating in the *Mode of Pretense*. Pretense is used by almost everyone to get what they want in situations where being honest and open would be risky and potentially unsuccessful. We say that we would not have a working society were it not for the skillful practice of pretense. Before we go further in this examination of how people get what they want through manipulating the perceptions of others, let's make very clear exactly what we are talking about.

In the Foreground, acts of pretense come in two varieties – *active* and *passive*. Active pretense includes flattery, dissemblance, exaggeration, diplomacy, and other acts of commission that are lies. A *lie* is a communication that *intentionally* misrepresents factual reality. This is distinct from a **mistake**, which is a communication that *accidentally* misrepresents factual reality. A classic example of human nature is the situation in which a lie is found out, and then the liar lies about having lied, stating that he made a mistake. This pretending not to pretend is the essence of the Mode of Pretense.

Passive instances of pretense include withheld criticisms, withheld opinions, and other acts of omission that conceal relevant facts or your real intent from the target of the pretense. An **omission** is anything not communicated so as to survive a perceived threat, to control, or to manipulate the listener.

Both active and passive uses of pretense come in three different types: white lies and omissions, other-serving lies and omissions, self-serving lies and omissions. **White lies and omissions** are those that are intended to smooth social interactions. For instance, when people ask, "How are you?" they are not usually interested in your condition. When you answer, "Fine," you are omitting all the facts that would be an accurate answer to the question, e.g., your cat just died and you were involved in a car accident on the way in to work today. The purpose of the interchange is to initiate a conversation and leave the questioner with the impression that you have your act together. An example of a white omission is not telling someone with whom you are dining that she has broccoli stuck in her teeth, so as to avoid mutual embarrassment.

Other-serving lies and omissions are the second type of pretense. Other serving lies are acts that are intended to benefit others. Examples include answering, "You look great!" when asked, "Do these clothes make me look fat?" or telling a child that he has what it takes to excel at a sport when you know it is not true, so that he will give his best effort and not lose self-esteem. An example of an other-serving omission is not sharing a serious diagnosis with family members so as to spare them worry and stress.

Other-serving pretense is also done professionally. Professional acting, for instance, is done in service to art and entertainment. Actors are pretending to be someone else, but they are not pretending not to pretend. We know that they are not the characters they play. They have studied for decades to master the art of pretending as a medium of creative expression. They undergo all the same stresses that other performing artists experience but also gain the benefits of creating something beautiful or meaningful. For them, the Mode of Pretense becomes the Art of Pretense. What they want to get from the audience, the target of their pretense, is delight, wonder, awe, applause, and recognition.

Self-serving lies and omissions are pretentious acts that are intended to benefit the pretender. These are the types of lies that we are ashamed of, or justify to ourselves, and which we have been taught are immoral. These self-serving lies and omissions are the ones that get us into trouble legally, personally, professionally, and spiritually. Examples of self-serving lies include padding your résumé, withholding information on a first date, sandbagging your sales results, cooking the books, adultery, and so on.

Espionage and diplomacy are forms of professional pretense that are done in service to king and country. Spies and diplomats sometimes operate behind enemy lines at great risk to themselves, pretending to be people they are not, to gain information about enemies and potential threats to their nations. From the intelligence professional's point of view, it is pretense done in service to "my people" and therefore justified and done without any loss of power. And yet it is a form of low intensity warfare in which operatives are constantly exposed to danger in hostile environments. It takes tremendous fortitude and skill not to get caught, killed, or arrested and to sustain that over a long period of time. The spy or diplomat is acting in many ways similar to a performing artist, but the purpose and the stakes are quite different. As an agent of a sovereign entity, the spy or diplomat executes on the war-like intention of that entity. The stresses and costs of this work are the same as with self-serving pretense even though the individual operative is performing in service to something greater than himself.

The High Cost of Pretense

Operating in the Mode of Pretense is the same as being at war with the target of your pretense. It requires constant vigilance and high intelligence to do it successfully. You have to remember everything you said in the past to maintain the pretense. You may get what you want in the near term, but there is always a price to pay. You create a hostile environment because pretending separates you from your target and your true self. It is impossible to commune with a person to whom you are pretending because the whole point is to conceal what is really going on with you so as to manipulate your target. What's worse, your moment-to-moment behaviors are determined by the responses of your target. To be successful in getting what you want, you must constantly react to the moves of your target. And ironically, your body language cannot pretend. Your eyes betray a fake smile. Your breathing, voice, behavior, and posture invariably point to your duplicity. And yet, people habitually pretend with each other all the time.

Discovering that you are the target of someone's pretense provokes all kinds of negative emotions and vengeful thoughts. Think of a time when you discovered that you were being "played" or lied to. The anger at the betrayal of trust, the sting of embarrassment at discovering you had been fooled, the obsessive thoughts of how to defend yourself and somehow prevail, all take you over, make your day miserable, and leave you disheartened or bitter.

To summarize the experience of the Mode of Pretense, the intent in the Background is to get what you want by misrepresenting your actual point of view or intent. Your purpose is to manipulate your target through speaking and acting.

The focus of your attention while speaking and acting is on the reactions of your target. When you listen in this mode, you listen for advantage and opportunity as a suspicious adversary would. The Midground experience of operating in the Mode of Pretense includes constant vigilance, thoughts driven by the responses of your target, fear, guilt, shame, anger, *schadenfreude*, an experience of tunnel vision, dilated sense of time, and exaggerated stress symptoms.

There are benefits to operating in Pretense. It allows you to spare people's feelings, manipulate results, and lubricate social interactions. The costs of operating in this mode are that it requires constant vigilance, creates a hostile environment, separates you from others, compromises self-integration, and saps your energy.

Pretense is natural

All animals play the part of the trickster to get what they want. Consider the flounder lying at the bottom of the ocean. It camouflages itself by burrowing under the sand, leaving only its eyes protruding so it can see prey approaching. The flounder pretends to be the ocean floor. When a likely meal approaches, it lunges explosively at its prey, achieving its intended outcome. Many animals and plants use camouflage to survive.

For human beings, the Mode of Pretense is like camouflage. We use it to survive a perceived threat or when we are confronted with a demand for change. We manipulate the perceptions of our targets to achieve our intended results. Pretense actually works, although it may not be very useful in building a high performance team or when cultivating trust between people. Pretense can be appropriate but it is also limiting.

To do pretense well requires the ability to read another person's mind. This is why your four year old is such a poor liar. To pretend successfully, we need to have a mental model of the target's mind so that we can accurately predict his responses. This kind of cognitive complexity doesn't arise in people until they are age seven or older. The ability to lie well is strongly correlated to leadership ability. This is not because leaders need to be liars, but because reading the true Background intentions of people is necessary to inspire and motivate them to take effective action.

Pretense is not a moral question; it's not about good or bad. It's how, in the real world, people get what they want when they are afraid, or when they perceive that they have no direct control. We were told as very young children not to lie. And yet, when at age five you said, "Look at the fat person, mama!" you were told to not say that. This is a very confusing situation for a young mind. In our religious training we are taught that lying is evil, and yet we see it done frequently by our parents, our teachers, and other authority figures. When you were fifteen years old, did you always tell your parents everything you were doing? Most adolescents lie and withhold as required to get their ways. By that age, we had figured out how to get what we want even though we had no worldly power or resources. If, as adults, we base our success in the world on living a life of pretense, we run the risk of losing all sense of reality, our sense of ourselves, and the possibility of ever being truly happy and fulfilled.

If we take power to mean the ability to manifest our intentions in reality at high velocity, operating in the Mode of Pretense is the most powerless one can be. That is because in pretense, the pretender makes each next move based on the reactions of others. It's all about causing a certain appearance. It's about manipulating people through controlling their impressions. If you had real power, you would cause the results you want by virtue of your saying so. People who take the point of view that they don't have what it takes to get what they need, or can't express themselves more openly, use the Mode of Pretense to get what they want.

Think On This

How do you use The Mode of Pretense to get what you want at work? What has it cost you and your loved ones when you have operated in the Mode of Pretense?

If you didn't have to pretend to get what you want, how would you go about it?

• Write these insights down.

Insights

Insights

NOTE: After getting acquainted with the Modes of Argument and Pretense and their negative effects on both individuals and groups, you may be feeling a little uncomfortable. Being reminded of the dark side of humanity is not pleasant. If you recognized that you often default to these Modes yourself, as others do, you may be finding it hard to concentrate or even to understand what you are reading. Your mind doesn't want to look where your attention is being directed.

The next chapter reveals even more confronting concepts that uncover how we unwittingly undermine our own and others' leadership, creativity, and power. We recommend that you consciously choose to discover the reality of your own human operating system. Relief and new possibilities will come soon.

On Being Powerless

We have distinguished three Modes of Intention so far: Presentation, Argument, and Pretense. Most people are operating in these modes most of the time. A semantic analysis of the recorded conversations in a typical corporate meeting room will show that about ninety-eight per cent (98%) of the conversations are held in these three modes, the majority being held in the Mode of Presentation, followed by Argument and Pretense.

What is the impact on an organization when the whole workforce is operating in these three modes, almost all the time? Where is the focus of people's attention? They are mostly attending to themselves, their opinions, and getting what they want through skillful manipulation. Results, when they occur, seem to happen almost randomly. Everyone in the group is attending to his or her neighbors assessing, "Is this politically correct? Will my stock move up or down if I say this thing?" Because they see the world through the filters of the Mode of Argument without even knowing it, they are all working on solving problems, not delivering, creating, or innovating. They speak and listen to collect agreement for their points of view thus a lot of energy is spent on finding people who agree with them, collecting evidence, and successfully making arguments in meetings. Very little valuable work is getting done. Power is lost in an organization where this condition is the norm. This is how human beings at the conventional level of development work together when they operate in groups.

People spend a lot of time writing e-mails in these organizations. Because open and honest communication is not practiced, many hours are spent crafting skillfully worded e-mails to make sure they are going to be received properly, considering how to say what should be said, and avoiding what should not be said. They ask themselves, "What is politically correct?" and "Is this going to tweak somebody if I say it this way?" It is a huge waste of time and effort. Because e-mails carry no tonal or gestural information, the text is often misinterpreted due to people filtering the information through Mode of Argument and Mode of Pretense lenses. And none of that work is actually about doing something valuable for the business.

Most leadership and management books, seminars, and trainings are designed to train people to produce tangible results in this conventional environment. Not much changes after that training, because the leaders are not addressing the actual causative factors. People cannot think outside of the three modes until they learn to think, listen, and speak differently.

These ways of operating as humans are automatic and programmed during your formative years. They are a part of your cultural DNA. Even as a small child, these modes of intention are occurring. As a leader, you cannot mandate that people stop pretending at work. You can't mandate that people stop complaining at work. What you can do is to have people become aware of the costs and the benefits of the modality they are in. You can help them gain the awareness that, "Gee, I am trying to get something done but I am embedded in this other mode that has nothing to do with getting anything done. No wonder I can't make it happen." When that realization occurs, a new way of living life becomes available and things begin to change for the better for everyone involved.

Justification, Excuses, and Blame

Before we can move to the alternatives for these ways of operating, we will look at the organizational impact of people working together in these three modes of intention. If everyone around you is opining, arguing, and pretending, sharing the point of view that something is wrong around here, and believing he or she is powerless to change the circumstances, then a culture of powerlessness develops. People say, "I can't get my job done because 'the circumstances' won't allow it." (In place of "the circumstances," insert any situation outside of myself to which I can assign the blame for my failure). If the workers say that they are not responsible for the results because of the circumstances, then the managers tell the executives, "We can't be responsible for the results because of the workers." Then the executives say to the Board of Directors, "We can't be responsible for the results because the managers can't get their jobs done." Then the Board tells the investors, "Current market conditions and changes in performance require that we adjust expectations for the second half of the fiscal year." If everyone up and down the organization is not responsible for the results, then who is actually running the company? No one!

"It's not whether you win or lose. It's how well you place the blame." – Ralph Kiner, baseball great

There are always outliers in any organization – people who are generative, resourceful, optimistic, and creative. They are the twenty per cent (20%) that produce eighty per cent (80%) of the results. But in most organizations, the conventional rank and file members of the team who habitually live in the Modes of Presentation, Argument, and Pretense outnumber them and actively suppress their influence. It will be useful, and ultimately very profitable, for us to understand the worldview of people who consider themselves powerless in the face of "the circumstances."

Victimhood

Someone who thinks of him or herself that way could be called a victim. A victim is a person who has no choice in the matter of the circumstances and has no ability to change them. From this perspective, power is not available to manifest your intent with and through people. No matter what you do, you are powerless to alter the situation. People who look at the world through these lenses continually repeat that they are helpless, tell likely stories about why this is so, and enlist other people in sharing their points of view. Their stories are substitutes for the results expected of them. They cannot be held accountable for their failures because, in their current reality, they sincerely tried very hard, but the circumstances were insurmountable. This way of looking at things is at the root of every stuck problem on the planet. "We can't have peace because 'they' won't 'let us.'" "I can't have what I want because the he/she/it isn't the way he/she/it should be and I can't do anything about it." The fundamental point of view of a victim is "The situation is bigger than I am and I have no ability to respond to it." "Woe is me."

Argument With Reality

There is a way of viewing the world consistent with being a victim called having an ***Argument with Reality***. It surfaces when a person is faced with a perceived threat to her identity or when a PMA has been triggered. When a person has an argument with reality, he or she becomes deeply embedded in the Mode of Argument. Everything is seen through the filter of "something's wrong and I'm right about that." It's a form of delusion. It's as though you lived in Seattle and you complained for years about the wet weather and the cold saying, "It shouldn't be this way. This is just terrible." But you know what? It is that way and your assertions that it shouldn't be that way are irrational. Why? Because it actually is that way in reality. If you don't like the weather where you live, your options are to adapt, move, or continue to complain. The weather is not negotiable; it might change, but it is not subject to your will. Maintaining your persistent complaint about the weather will not change anything in reality, but that is consistent with the point of view that you, the victim, have no power to alter the circumstances.

Now apply this notion to being a victim of circumstance in business. If you strongly hold the point of view that, "Our leader is terrible. He should be a wiser, more capable leader, but he acts incompetently. He shouldn't be that way." Then by promoting the strongly held point of view "He shouldn't be that way" you make yourself and others miserable about how the leader should be.

You might be right about the facts of the matter and yet you keep asserting over and over and over again that it should be some other way. A victim of circumstance would never realize the fundamental absurdity in the persistent complaint because he can't see it any other way. It all looks very real to the victim. He would rather maintain his strongly held point of view about what should be, rather than take action to change the situation. He would rather be right, than happy and successful.

Why would an otherwise sane person hold this self-defeating point of view? Why would someone, who in other parts of his or her life is quite effective, find himself or herself maintaining a delusional argument with reality about a particular situation? Consider that there might be a hidden benefit in doing so. It's a self-fulfilling prophecy and a perfect excuse for nonperformance.

For example, a salesperson in financial services may express a persistent complaint such as, "You know those dopey investment bankers we have to work with? They are slick, incompetent, slow-moving con artists who never deliver on what they say. No wonder I can't make my target. Look what I have to work with!" In this person's world, the reason he can't make his numbers is because of a circumstance outside his control. It really looks that way to him, and he can't imagine the situation being different. It may be factually true that the particular investment bankers he is working with are unreliable louts, but it never occurs to him that he could have a say in the matter and change the situation.

Since, in the Mode of Argument, he is driven to promote his strongly held point of view as "The Truth," he takes action by making a case for how incompetent and untrustworthy the investment bankers are. If he succeeds in convincing himself and his listeners, he will have successfully excused his lack of results and avoided the blame. He will have gotten off the hook for delivering and perhaps even receive some sympathy for his situation. By convincing himself and others that the investment bankers are the reason for his inability to produce, he may appear to be admirable to some by virtue of criticizing the integrity of the investment bankers. He may get sympathy, but most importantly, the fear of being held to account for delivering on his commitment will be temporarily relieved because he is not the source of the failure. There is clearly a lot of psychological benefit (secondary gains) in sticking to his strongly held point of view.

He may receive those benefits, but as with everything in life, costs come with these benefits. Because he is internally conflicted by the crossed purposes of making his target and avoiding risk and loss of status due to failure, he suffers stress symptoms such as persistent back problems, gastrointestinal discomfort, insomnia, and lack of sex drive. His loses peace of mind and the experience of happiness due to constant worry, anger and resentment. In prosecuting his gossip campaign against the investment bankers, he may be perceived as petty, untrustworthy, and unappealing by his coworkers, thus ironically undermining his instinctual intent to be liked and admired. But perhaps most importantly, by holding on to that point of view, he unwittingly robs himself of the power to change the circumstances. He has substituted a likely story for his ability to produce results and has traded his power and integrity for the hope of deflecting accountability.

Here is the really delusional part of this: He doesn't know that he holds a point of view in the Background.

What's going on in the Background is unconscious to him by definition. The way the situation appears, it's completely real to him. It's just how the world seems when he is embedded in the persistent pretentious argument that his Background psychology is perpetrating on his conscious self. His unconscious Background is presenting a skillfully filtered version of reality to his conscious Midground, and there is no way for him to discover that. He is totally justified and completely right in his view. There is no hope.

Getting Your Power Back

All humans have the freedom to make fundamental choices about how they will face the circumstances of their lives. The question is, "Will I take personal responsibility for the way I approach these difficult circumstances?" Assuming that you are mentally well and possess your human faculties, you have the capacity to do that. Said in another way, you can decide to "make your own luck."

It's possible, by virtue of your ability to choose your attitude in any set of circumstances, to shift the filters in the Background from Powerless to Powerful. You can give yourself the authority to have a say in how the situation turns out simply by declaring it so. In reality, the facts of the matter will not change. They are what they are, independent of anyone's opinions, feelings, or point of view. The facts are not the problem. The problem is your insistence on maintaining a delusional Argument with Reality that provides you hidden psychological benefits, yet costs you power, health, and happiness.

If you choose to change your mind, to stop arguing with Reality, and to take responsibility for getting what you want, you can begin to imagine what actions could be taken to start influencing the circumstances. You begin to think about whom you could ask for assistance, what plans need to be made, and whose approval is required. After choosing to be powerful instead of powerless, you could begin to see where you have direct control and what you might do with that control.

Making the choice to change your mind like that is not easily done without training. The choice can happen when you tell the truth to yourself about how you've been, the negative impact your behavior has had on you and others, and after forgiving yourself for being so stubbornly attached to such a counterproductive point of view. Once learned and practiced, you can master yourself over time and begin to create a future that is free from the negative effects of self-defeating Background processes.

Dealing with Reality

There are some situations in life over which we have little or no influence. The time of our death, the politics of other countries, the vagaries of the markets, and the weather are good examples. If a problem arises similar to, "I want to have a long and happy life, but a large asteroid will impact Earth and cause an extinction event in two weeks time," then you will still have a choice in the matter of what to do with the rest your life. You could spend all your time in the situation arguing that it's unfair and tragic. This tack will not change the circumstances and will leave you unhappy and disempowered. Or you could choose to be responsible and spend your remaining days in a way that makes the last two weeks a "long and happy" time. This approach would give you a completely different experience and is consistent with the truth that our lives are finite. I recommend the latter approach.

Steven Covey invented a very useful tool for delineating Spheres of Control, Influence, and Concern. We have a limited number of things that we can control directly. In the Sphere of Control, we can directly change the circumstances at will. Our Sphere of Control is a subset of a larger domain of life called our Sphere of Influence. In the Sphere of Influence, we have access to the people who have direct control over the circumstances. Through using our leadership skills and abilities, we can exercise personal power to change the circumstances by influencing those people. Finally, in the Sphere of Concern, there is a universe of circumstances in life about which we are care but over which we have no influence or direct control. For example, I might be concerned about people going hungry around the world. In my current state, I may have no direct control or influence in the matter. If I choose to respond to the world hunger problem, I could take actions that would increase my influence in the matter, like joining a not-for-profit company whose mission is to end world hunger. This would move world hunger from my Sphere of Concern to my Sphere of Influence. Alternatively, I could, after reflection, choose to leave world hunger in my Sphere of Concern and pick a different pathway to express my personal power and make a difference.

The things that can be controlled and influenced become available when you notice that you are lying to yourself about your inability to control and influence the circumstances. Your declaration that you have a say in the matter of the future gives you power. While fundamentally audacious, that declaration is the birthright of every person and is the source of fulfillment in life.

Think On This

How has taking the point of view of a victim of circumstance personally cost you in your job and in your life?

What is a long-standing problem that you have for which you are now choosing to be responsible? What actions are you going to take to resolve it?

• Write down these possible actions and then by when you will have taken them.

• Share your plans with someone else.

• Then get to work fulfilling the future you say can happen.

Insights

Insights

The Source of Power

In the previous chapter you saw that once the choice has been made to actively respond to circumstances rather than be victimized by them, you can take actions that create what you want to have in the Foreground. This is an expression of power. Let's clearly distinguish what is meant by the word power.

In normal parlance, **power** is often used to mean control or domination as in the ability to manipulate the circumstances or people to your will. This ordinary way of thinking comes from the habitual Modes of Argument and Pretense; wherein, convincing someone to agree with you (winning against them) is a demonstration of superior *force*. To win a deal because you are the smartest, richest and most together guy in the room is a demonstration of force. To be able to conduct an orchestra because you are smarter and more politically savvy than the members of the orchestra, can hear every mistake, and know ten times more about music than anyone else is a demonstration of force.

You can start to see that *force* is common. It's the prevailing paradigm. Often, when people try to make things happen in the world, they try using force to change the circumstances. This approach is usually a very heavy lift. When is the last time that you tried to force someone to change how he or she thinks? How did that turn out? Trying to get people to change their points of view by force is very difficult. It takes a long time and a lot of emotional energy. Figuratively you beat them around the head and ears with rubber hoses to make it happen. The Way of Force involves getting what you want by manipulating or dominating people and the environment. It results in unintended consequences and reactive fear-driven human beings. Force is just ordinary.

Power is not force. Power, in the sense we are using the word, is "power to..." not "power over..." What we mean by power is the ability to manifest your intentions in reality with velocity. What does velocity mean? Velocity has two dimensions – direction and speed. A person operating with power is someone who is taking effective actions that have a clear direction at high speed. The results produced by these actions are exactly what the person intended to produce in the Foreground.

Let's say that you declare the intention to move to a new city and buy a house. If you make that declaration on a Sunday afternoon, and one week later you are signing the deed for your new house, you could say that you demonstrated high power. You were able to manifest your intention in reality with high velocity. If, however, you made that same declaration on Sunday afternoon and then three months later you had just begun to look for a new house, we would assess that you took action to fulfill your intention but at a much lower level of power than the one week example of the project. By this definition, ultimate power would be the ability to say "X" and have "X" show up in reality a moment later. The Biblical declaration "*Let there be light. And there was light."* in Genesis 1:3 is an example of ultimate creative power.

Power is creative, not destructive. It's attractive, not driving. Power causes win-win scenarios naturally. There is no blowback from the exercise of real power. There is satisfaction and fulfillment for everyone involved. Power is the ability to create the circumstances you want by expressing your natural integrity in the world. And here is the surprise: by exercising power in service to a high purpose, you also serve yourself and are rewarded for that.

Integrity

We say that the source of power for human beings is integrity. To understand what this word means for individuals and for organizations, we'll introduce a very ancient model for the design of human beings that has become part of the perennial philosophy first articulated in the Vedas and reflected through Plato and all the subsequent enlightenment systems that have arisen over several thousands of years. To make the model practical and relevant to the 21st century, we will use a simplified version of it without the cultural overlay that comes with its history.

This model can be understood in terms of the functions of various aspects of the human being going from the most primitive to the most abstract and complex. We will distinguish six different dimensions of human beings that together make up a complete integrated whole.

The first dimension is the ***physical*** body including the parts of the brain that control its basic functions. This is the dimension of the five senses and includes all the auto-

113

matic functions operating in the Background that govern metabolism, reproduction, healing, and maintaining the homeostasis of the body. It exists in the Foreground as well as providing the Midground experience of body sensations.

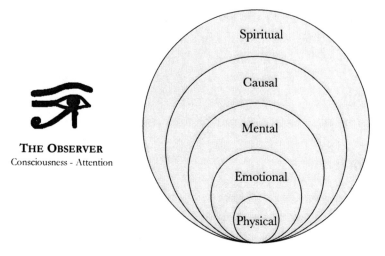

THE OBSERVER
Consciousness - Attention

Figure 6: The Dimensions of Human Being

The second dimension is the ***emotional*** aspect of self. This dimension gives us the Midground experience of feelings like anger, fear, shame, and guilt, as well as love, joy, passion, and belonging. The associated brain structure is the limbic system and the Background medium is the physio-chemical system and processes associated with emotional experience and expression.

The third dimension is the ***mental*** aspect of self. It self-generates the thoughts and images that run through the Midground experience. This is the realm of abstract concept and meaning making activities. It includes all our memories and the stories we construct to organize them into meaningful structures that make our identities homeostatic.

The fourth dimension is the *causal* aspect of the self. This is the source of intentionality – the will to choose and act on our choice. It is the part of the Background that causes our actions and directs our attention.

The fifth dimension of self is the *spiritual* layer of human being. In this context, spirit is used to mean the aspects of self in the Background that underlie a person's core values, purpose, and true passions in life. Since these aspects of self are at the source of who you are, this layer informs and motivates all the previous layers.

The sixth and final dimension of human beings is called *The Observer*. The Eye of Horus in Egyptian history was the symbol for this most subtle aspect of human being. The Observer is the pure unadulterated field of consciousness that witnesses the action in all the other layers of being. It has no qualities, characteristics, or functions other than being the space in which everything else occurs. Said differently, it's the part of self that allows you to experience your experience.

For most people, the spiritual, causal, and even mental layers of the self are unavailable to awareness. Our purpose, values, and passions that drive our intentions are in the Background. For people that have suffered psychological trauma, some thoughts, emotions, and memories are also unavailable due to the mind suppressing them. In extreme cases, people have hysterical blindness to anything too closely associated with the source of the trauma. A person in this condition is deeply fragmented and has little power to alter the circumstances. Healing work is required to restore his or her natural integrity.

Being Integrated

When you develop enough skill to become aware of your purpose, your intentions, your thoughts, and your emotions, you then have the ability to choose what you are for, what you intend, what you are thinking and feeling, and what you are doing to fulfill your purpose. A person like that is functioning with power. This is what is meant by integrity – the alignment of purpose, intention, thought, feeling, action, and Foreground results that, if delivered, fulfill the declared purpose. Every aspect of the self is directed and aligned to fulfill one inspiring purpose.

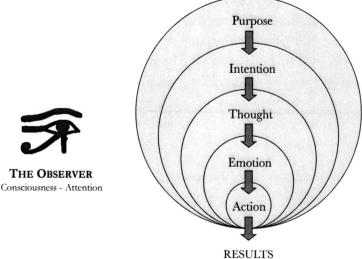

Figure 7: Being Integrated

To understand what being integrated looks and feels like, imagine a time when you were doing exactly what you wanted to be doing, getting the results you wanted without effort, without impediments, and you experienced a state of flow. Some people describe skiing down a slope in fresh powder or surfing a perfect wave in those terms.

116

The action and the actor are one. There is no anxiety and little sense of time passing. You are fully present, alive, and engaged. The Midground is very quiet and filled with positive emotions and vivid connection to the Foreground.

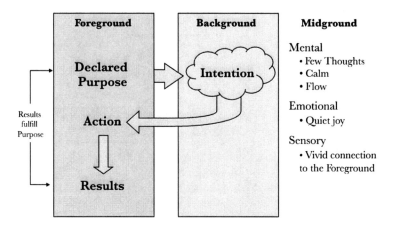

Figure 8: Being Integrated as a Process

The illustration above describes the state of being integrated. You have declared a purpose to fulfill in the Foreground. Your commitment to that purpose gives you an intention in the Background that drives your actions. The actions naturally produce results that fulfill the purpose. As usual, your Midground is along for the ride experiencing a pleasant flow state. It's really quiet.

Being in an integrated state is usually the exception in life. Most often, in real world situations, we have conflicting intentions in the Background that cause us to become fragmented and to lose power. This is not a moral flaw. It's the natural state of things.

For example, you may have chosen to build your business to three times its size in the next three years. You think

117

this is a worthy purpose because when it's accomplished you will have a lot more money and freedom. It sounds fine, but because you are a human animal with primal instincts, you also have a default purpose to avoid risk, to be comfortable, and to avoid the domination of others.

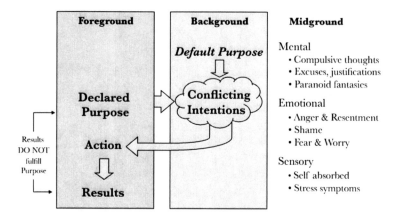

Figure 9: Being Fragmented as a Process

As you set about doing the work to build your business, you may find yourself struggling to produce the results you need to produce. The actions you must take to triple the size of your business require you to take risks, to be uncomfortable, and to be dominated by the job and the circumstances surrounding the growth. Your default purpose to be comfortable and your declared purpose to be successful are in conflict. This gives you opposing intentions in the Background that produce ineffective actions in the Foreground. This fragmented state gives you a Midground experience filled with paranoid fantasies, excuses and justifications, compulsive thoughts, self-deception, negative emotions, self-absorption, and physical stress.

Because this situation is so uncomfortable, you oscillate back and forth between taking effective but difficult actions and avoiding them so that you can fulfill your animal need to be comfortable and stay safe. You are internally fragmented and the fragmentation robs you of the power you could have if you served only one high purpose. What's worse is that this is all happening in the Background so you are unaware of the source of your difficulties.

Often your default purpose is to fulfill your desires or to maintain your current identity. You have appetites and addictions to having things, or feeling certain ways, or to being right about strongly held points of view that can conflict with the purposes you choose to fulfill. For most people, being comfortable, looking good, and surviving perceived threats are the default purposes in the Background much of the time. This is not a problem in itself. It is only a problem if you deceive yourself about it.

Robert Fritz, the author of many books on creativity and the determinacy of structure, invented the notion of a **_structural conflict_** that is useful in understanding being fragmented and the power loss associated with it. In a structural conflict, opposing intentions create an oscillating structure that inhibits forward progress towards fulfilling a purpose.

If we take the common case of someone trying to lose weight, the idea becomes very clear. You have a declared purpose to decrease the amount of fat in your body. You also have a default purpose as a human animal to be emotionally and physically comfortable. The two exist together and produce conflicting intentions that cause your behavior to oscillate between taking effective actions to lose weight and taking effective actions to make yourself comfortable.

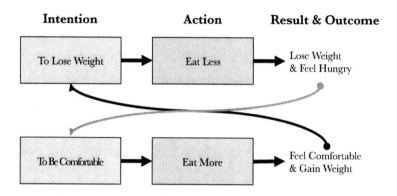

Figure 10: Example of a Structural Conflict

There is no way to resolve this oscillating system if both purposes are equally important. The lack of fulfilling results for either purpose is an inevitable reality of the inherent conflict between them. This is the primary reason why people have a hard time losing weight on their own.

Structural conflicts arise in every field of endeavor. In finance, the purpose to invest money conflicts with the purpose to avoid risk. In building a business, the purpose to expand and grow conflicts with the purpose to be comfortable and stay the same. At more fundamental human levels, the purpose to connect and intimately relate to people conflicts with the purpose to remain free and distinctly yourself. The notion of structural conflict is very useful for sorting out the reality of why people can be ineffective while trying so hard to be successful.

The way to resolve a structural conflict is to choose to make one of the purposes more important than the other.

When you are willing to do what it takes to lose weight, even if it means you will be uncomfortable from time to time, you will make progress toward fulfilling that purpose. The conscious choice to value one purpose higher than the other allows for the cessation of oscillating results and for making forward progress.

A key question for leaders who are up to fulfilling high purposes is, "How uncomfortable are you willing to be to fulfill your purpose?" Can you be comfortable with being uncomfortable in service to something that is truly your heart's desire? Anytime you take on something that requires more from you than you already have, you will need to change yourself to accomplish it. Changing yourself is always painful in some way at some level of self. Are you willing to do the work so that your declared purpose is fulfilled? Choosing the higher purpose will allow you to integrate yourself fully and give you the experience of joy, freedom, and flow while manifesting your intentions in reality with high velocity.

You may have noticed that New Year's resolutions go by the wayside in a matter of days for most people. Not enough willpower exists to sustain a personal change initiative over time. The same effect happens with corporate initiatives. Eventually, you forget that you are working on the project. It disappears in the stream of daily activities and is forgotten.

A structure of partnership and commitment allows for keeping yourself integrated and effective over time no matter how substantial the change you are working on producing. By declaring your purpose to another person who is willing to hold you to account for fulfilling it, and then finding another stakeholder who will assist you when the going gets rough, you can avoid the structural conflicts associated with change and operate with high power in fulfilling your dreams.

Think On This

Where in your leadership practice have you used force? What were the unintended outcomes, good and bad, that arose from that application of force?

Where in your life can you replace force with real power? What will you do to increase your integrity in those areas?

- Write these areas down with what you will do to integrate yourself.

- What are the structural conflicts in your personal and professional life that you would like to resolve?

- Write them out using Figure 10 as an example. Which intentions will you choose to have higher priority?

Insights

Insights

The Mode of Execution

We saw in the previous chapter how integrity is the source of power. When people truly intend to manifest a result in the world, their thinking, emotions, physical state, and actions all align on making that result happen. From an external point of view, they can look almost superhuman because of the uncommon way they move through the world creating ways around the obstacles presented by the circumstances. From a normal person's perspective, the intended results show up as if by magic.

This kind of high performance is relatively easy to understand on an individual level. Smart successful people strive for years to get the knowledge, skills, connections, resources, and results they need to fulfill their visions. If they are serving a purpose greater than their own self-interest, they will have the energy and focus to produce amazing results even in difficult circumstances. The pathway is not so clear if you consider how one would lead a whole team or community into the extraordinary space of high performance. If you consider that your job as a leader is to imagine, communicate, and deliver on an inspiring future for the group by causing aligned effective actions in people, then the territory is not so obvious.

To get a more experiential understanding of what high-level group performance looks like, we can take an example from the world of the performing arts. The symphonic orchestra has often been used as a metaphor for teamwork, business, and leadership. The problem in making this metaphor useful is that most people have no clue what the orchestra's leader, the conductor, actually does and how he or she accomplishes it. Let's unpack the metaphor a bit to get a few layers down, where we can see how the orchestra and its leadership job might apply to leading other kinds of groups.

Imagine standing in front of a group of about one hundred seated people around you, all of whom are as smart, or smarter, than you. They are all first-tier masters in their profession and have multiple degrees, decades of experience, and qualifications to prove it. They each have strong opinions about how things should go and maybe about how able you are as a leader. Most of them believe that they could lead the orchestra better than you. And they are all listening in the Mode of Argument by default, as do most people.

The orchestra is seated in a semi-circle covering a distance of fifty feet, left to right, and forty feet, back to front. They have sheet music in front of them, similar to the script for a play, which contains their individual parts for the notes they will play. Even though they are masters of their instruments, they cannot just start playing together. Because there are so many of them, they can't start simultaneously unless someone gives them a visual command that shows when to start and precisely how fast the music will go. That's the first job of the conductor − to set the speed of the music and to align each person's actions perfectly so that all are synchronized.

Once the music has started, the second job of the conductor is to shape and sculpt the sound of the music by giving visual and verbal directions to the instrumentalists during rehearsal and by only visual commands in performance. The players themselves cannot align without direction because getting one hundred people exactly aligned on how to inflect a phrase or nuance a note is almost impossible by consensus. Remember that they all have amazing credentials and strong opinions. To make rehearsal time efficient and cost effective, the musicians empower a conductor to provide the aesthetic and tactical direction.

To be successful leading this high-powered group, what does the conductor have to provide? You may remember that the source of action is intention. Intention always precedes action. The job of the conductor is to perfectly align the intentions of one hundred complicated people so that they play exactly together and inflect the music in exactly the same way. What does it take to accomplish that?

What it takes is laser beam focused, coherent, highly intentional communication. There can be no doubt or wavering in the mind of the conductor, or else the mixed intentions in his Background will show up in the Foreground through his gestural language. (Experienced musicians can tell instantly if a conductor is pretending or just not clear.) He must be so clear in his intentions that every person watching is also absolutely certain and confident about what to do and when to do it. Further, the conductor must win the respect of the orchestra by consistently demonstrating that his or her vision is beautiful, strong, specific, and worth serving. The purpose that he or she is fulfilling is not self-aggrandizement or any other individual motive.

It is a purpose of all orchestra musicians – to create and share mind-arresting timeless moments of delight, wonder, and awe.

If we apply the example of the orchestra to business, what do we find? What does it take to get one hundred really smart, highly educated and experienced professionals, who all think that they know how it should go and have strong opinions about everything, to align their intentions and execute in synchrony to fulfill a shared purpose with high performance? Not surprisingly, it takes the same kind of intentional leadership that a conductor brings to leading an orchestra. It takes laser beam focused, coherent, highly intentional communication to have people's actions all align. The work activity and work product are different. The leadership challenge is the same.

The Mode of Execution

When leaders use language to cause coordinated action with people, they are operating in the *Mode of Execution*. Speaking and listening in the Mode of Execution causes effective action and commitment in people by aligning their intentions.

Here is an example of how it works. If I say to you, "Hey Reader, *how about if* we have dinner sometime?" you might respond back with "Sure. Sounds good." If at this point in the conversation we leave the topic of having dinner together, do we share a clear expectation that we have date for dinner? No, we don't. We've only expressed a desire to do so, but our intentions are not aligned on actually making it happen.

If I say to you, "Hey Reader, *could* we have dinner together some time?" you might respond with, "Yes, we could." If the conversation goes no further than this, do we share a commitment to have dinner together? No, we don't. All that has happened is that I have inquired about your ability to have dinner with me and you have responded that you are capable of doing that. You have not committed to anything in the future.

If, however, I say to you, "Hey Reader, ***will you*** have dinner with me ***tomorrow night at 6:30 p.m. at Harrigan's?***" something very different happens in your Background. As soon as you hear that question asked that way, your Background automatically goes through an approximately 0.5 second process considering your availability, the feasibility, and the desirability of the invitation. Your Midground is very quiet for that short time until your Background comes up with an answer. If you feel that you actually have a choice in the matter and you choose to say yes, you might say, "Yes, I will." Do we now share a clear expectation about where we are going to be and what we are going to do tomorrow at 6:30 p.m.? Yes, we do. From now until then, assuming we are not pretending with each other, we will arrange our lives so that tomorrow at 6:30 p.m. we will meet at Harrigan's restaurant. Dinner is on.

In the Mode of Execution, the Background intention is to produce a result in the future. While speaking, your attention is on being clear and causing committed action. While listening, your attention is on looking for clarity, specificity, and feasibility. The benefits of this Mode of Intention are that it causes effective action and establishes clear accountability for results. Used properly, it can build trust and effectiveness on a high performance team. The possible drawbacks of operating in this mode are that it can be used to manipulate people, especially if they feel that they don't have a choice in the matter of a request or an offer.

The Midground content of a person in the Mode of Execution includes a sharp attention to detail and thoughts on implementation and feasibility. At the emotional level, people feel a sense of anticipation, certainty, and a tension and release as the alignment between people occurs. At the sensory level, people in this mode experience time standing still in moments of truth when commitments are made and the visual field is focused on the other person in the interchange. In the Foreground, the kinds of conversations you'll hear are negotiations that result in committed action, agreements being made, straight talk about delivery, acknowledgments of the actual results, and clear definitions of accountability.

The Mode of Execution is a fundamentally different kind of intentional space because the Background intent is to produce a tangible result in the future. It is speaking and listening with the intent to alter the circumstances in the Foreground by virtue of the speaker and listener taking purposeful action. There is no explanation, presentation, argument, or pretense. There is no attention on the past at all. There is only the intention to make and complete commitments. It is the way people talk when action is happening in business.

The Mode of Execution is about the shaping of expectations and the aligning of intentions. When a person asks for your commitment to deliver something in the future, you have a choice to align your intention with theirs so that you can accomplish something that serves both your interests. In a meeting where the majority of the conversation is in the Modes of Presentation, Argument, and Pretense, anyone can shift the meeting into action by changing the context of the conversation to one where action is called for. Applying the tools of Execution does this exceptionally well.

The Word "Will"

The most basic tool in the Mode of Execution is the word "will." Its use with the Background intention to cause a result in the future always causes committed action. Consider the illustration.

	Telling	**Asking**
Others act	You will… *<execute result.>*	Will you… *<execute result?>*
You act	I will… *<execute result.>*	Shall I… *<execute result?>*

Figure 11: Four uses of the word "Will"

In using the Mode of Execution you always have two parties – one is receiving the result, the other is providing the result. One party is initiating the action by either asking or telling the other party using one of four moves.

1) Telling someone that he will deliver a result sounds like: "Frank, I have a job for you. You will deliver the 10K

report at the Monday staff meeting next week. Any questions or concerns?" Giving a command like this requires that Frank has already given you permission to tell him what to do and requires his full understanding of the deliverable to be produced. These conditions normally exist in a military context or in other work environments where command and control are part of the culture.

2) Telling someone that you will deliver a result sounds like: "Frank, I will take on delivering the 10K report at the Monday staff meeting next week. You can take it off your list." Informing someone of your commitment to deliver a result in the future sets his or her expectations and makes you accountable to her or him to deliver it when you said you would. This is a great move for demonstrating leadership and initiative. It's also an excellent way to cause you to take actions that would be outside your comfort zone.

3) Asking people to choose if they will deliver a result sounds like: "Frank, will you please deliver the 10K report at the Monday staff meeting next week?" In this move, you are giving the party who will perform the actions and deliver the result a choice in the matter. If they perceive that they have the freedom to say no, then if they do say yes, it will be a real yes beyond mere compliance. You will actually have a committed partner bringing their best efforts to the work. For this reason, making requests is highly recommended when you are asking for results that are above and beyond business as usual. Asking in this way works well for causing action in people of all ages.

4) Asking someone to choose if you will deliver a result sounds like: "Frank, shall I deliver the 10K report at the Monday staff meeting next week?" In this move, you are

offering to provide the result if the other party would find value in that. Because you are involving the other party in the choice, he or she are very engaged in the interchange and can help set the specifications for the deliverable.

Asking Successfully

The conditions for asking successfully are:

1) ***There can be no pretense in the interchange***. If you want a person to take on doing something and get more of his energy and work spirit than mere compliance, you need to honestly ask him for it. This means that "no" has to be an acceptable answer. If it's not acceptable, then just tell him to do the task. If he is not within your Sphere of Control, then you need to bring your influencing skills to bear to try and get a "yes." But in no case can you pretend and manipulate if you want a person's best performance.

2) ***The performer has to understand exactly what you want and when you want it***. If you cannot clearly state the specifications for the result you want in terms that the other party understands, then you have no right to expect it. Often, due to unclear thinking, laziness or overwork, leader/managers give out vague assignments and ask for unspecific deliverables in unrealistic time frames. This lack of clarity and discipline causes large amounts of wasted time, rework, frustration, and damage to morale. It also costs the managers the respect of the people who report to them. It is demotivating to try to do a good job when the moving target is fuzzy.

3) ***There must be a Moment of Truth in the interchange***. Asking over e-mail is a setup for failure except

in work cultures that are already trained in the Mode of Execution and have strong relationships of accountability and trust. After sending off an e-mail, you have no idea if it's been read or if the person understands what you are asking. Far better to use tonal and gestural language cues to determine if a moment of commitment has happened for the other party. Connect and communicate if you wish to increase the probability of getting what you ask for.

The most basic skill of leadership is to know what you want and to be able to say it with vivid clarity for the listener. The importance of this cannot be overestimated. It is irritating and counterproductive to try to follow a person who is unclear about where he is going and what he wants. If you don't know what you want, you have no right to expect others to provide it. It is your responsibility as a leader and manager to be clear. Expecting people to read your mind, especially if you are unclear about it yourself, is the source of much waste, drama, and fear, and is at best wishful thinking.

How to Specify What You Want

There are two kinds of consequences of taking action in the real world – those that exist in physical reality and those that exist in the Midground or Background of people. We will call the Foreground kind a **result**.

A result is the physical effect of an action or series of actions that precede it. Results always exist in the Foreground, in both space and time. They are measurable, locatable, and have a beginning and ending in time. Results are visible to other people and exist independently of opinions, thoughts, and beliefs.

To reliably get the result you ask or tell people to provide, you need to skillfully specify it in language and clearly communicate it to them. Consider this example of what not to do when assigning a result to someone.

"Frank, we'd like you to ensure that we have a world-class marketing program here at Acme Corp. How does that sound to you?"

"Sure, Bob! That sounds like it's right up my alley."

"Very good. We'll check in at the end of the year and see how you're doing."

Not only is this example spoken in the Mode of Presentation requiring no alignment of intentions and no commitment from the performer of the task, it is impossible to execute. How could we measure if the marketing program is "world-class?" There is actually nothing for Frank to work on in reality except perhaps influencing Bob to think that the marketing program is indeed "world-class." At performance review time, what criteria will be used to determine if Frank got his job done? If Bob walks away from that interchange expecting great things, he is living in an illusory state. Consider the following request.

"Frank, will you be accountable for growing the marketing function this year so that by December 1 we are getting 100,000 independently verifiable impressions per month in our targeted web, print, and social media channels? This will be an increase of fifteen per cent (15%) over last year. Will you take that on?"

"I will, Bob. That is a project I can get excited about."

"Great! Thank you."

Specifying your intended result as an objectively measurable thing in the Foreground requires that you specifically state the way you will measure success in terms of a specific metric and then what quantity, standard of quality, exact size, level of detail, the delivery format, and the delivery time. While this may seem like a lot of work at first, it is far less wasteful than not getting what you want and having the costs of delay, rework, wasted materials and effort, opportunity costs, and the less tangible costs of irritated people who disrespect their manager's ability to communicate.

Specifying the time of delivery is a critical element without which there is no power in the interchange. Real things exist in both space and time. A powerful commitment to deliver a result can't happen unless the "by when" is specified. The acronym ASAP, while well meant by its users, is actually code for "whenever you get to it" because "as soon as possible" is not a time that can ever exist in reality. The performer of the task will not be compelled by integrity to organize his or her time around taking the actions to produce the result. A well-specified result always has a complete and accurate description of its specifications and a time by when it will be delivered in the future.

Outcomes

The internal human consequence of taking action is called an **outcome**. An outcome is the Midground or Background effect of a causative event that precedes it. Outcomes always exist in the Midground experience and Background potential of people. They are sensory, emotional, mental, intentional, or spiritual and are invisible until Foreground behavior changes to become consistent with the outcome. Outcomes alter or add to existing opinions, thoughts, and beliefs.

If you intend to produce a specific outcome with an individual person or a group of people, you can clarify and specify it by using the Dimensions of Human Being model. At the end of the process, what are the physical sensations you want them to have experienced? What are the emotions you want them to be feeling? What are the thoughts that you want them to be thinking? What knowledge do you want them to have that they didn't have before? What intentions or point of view do you want them to have? What purposes and values do you want them to adopt?

By getting clear on the outcomes you want to produce in people, you can design and manage conversations and other processes to produce those outcomes. To know if you achieved your intended outcomes, there must be some Foreground measurement of the outcome being produced.

If, for example, you were throwing a dinner party and your intended outcomes were that people leave happy, satisfied, and warmly related, you could measure that by noticing what people say to each other and how they relate to each other as they are getting ready to leave the party. Sincere expressions of affection and thanks for the evening accompanied by authentic body language cues will let you know if you achieved your outcomes.

In a workforce, you may wish to achieve a high standard of employee satisfaction. Real world measures of employee satisfaction could include low attrition rates, low number of sick days, expressions of gratitude and requests for further involvement from the workers, spontaneous expressions of happiness and social ease in the workplace, excellent survey results, and so on.

Designing and implementing conversations to execute results and produce favorable outcomes for people is the essence of the manager's job. Developing skill in the Mode of Execution, and its tools, is the path to delivering on the future that leadership envisions.

Think On This

Conversations in the Mode of Execution typically constitute only about one percent of all speaking and listening in most work places. If by intervening into the non-stop stream of Presentation, Argument, and Pretense, you can double that amount to two percent, you will have doubled the number of committed actions that are taken per unit of time.

> • Practice specifying what you want and asking people for it. Spend ten minutes at the beginning of each day crafting the "asks" and "tells" that you will accomplish that day. Then notice the acceleration of the results you and your people produce.

Insights

Insights

The Mode of Creation

Once you know how to say what you want with clarity for your listener and inspire committed action in them, you have the ability to cause effective action in yourself and others. Now you have a new problem: Where do you go to find out what to ask for? How do you stay ahead of the people you are leading? The skill of tactical leadership only empowers you to inspire commitment and produce results with others. It doesn't necessarily reveal what purpose to serve or the most important results to ask for.

Where you have to go to solve your new problem is the future. The ability to imagine a possible future and to articulate it so that others take action to fulfill that future is the job of a strategic leader. Strategic corporate leaders create and deliver on a future of increasing profit and shareholder value by causing effective actions with and through others. Creating and delivering on a future for your organization is at least a full time job and must be done well or your organization will be constrained by its past. Really.

The creative act of imagining a successful future and describing the best path to get there is a rare talent in the world, as we know. But it doesn't have to be inborn; it can be cultivated and that is the subject of this chapter.

Many of our institutions are led by loyal, hard working people who rose through the ranks of management due to their diligence and savvy. Now that they are at the top of an organization, the skills that got them there are not necessarily a match for the work they must do. They might know the organization's history, but can they envision its future? Does this sound familiar? The job is to create from nothing and then to manifest what you imagine through aligning the actions of others in the organization. How do you create something from nothing? For many people in positions of strategic leadership, the domain of real creativity is a new territory.

Organizational leadership is not the only context in which creativity is required. In fact, for any person to have a future that is filled with opportunity, learning to create possible futures is the key skill. Strategic leaders use it to rise above the status quo and triumph in the face of daunting challenges.

Let's get clear on what exactly is meant by the word create. To create is to bring something forth from nothing. Innovating is not creating. Innovating starts with a preexisting product, idea, or schema and then modifies it. Innovating comes from the Latin word *nova*, which means new. Innovation makes something new that already exists. To create means to bring something into existence starting with nothing.

How do you start with nothing? You have to suspend your constantly argumentative mind and let go of your continuous references to the past and your existing assumptions about the future. You begin with a truly blank canvas and then imagine what might possibly go there.

To get a sense of what creators do when they create, consider how a composer works. Moved by a mood, dream, insight, literary idea, or some other inspiration, a composer imagines music in her head that could be. How she does that is by grounding herself in the feeling or idea that has moved her and then listening into the silent void of her Background. Right at the interface between her conscious Midground and the deep silence of the unconscious Background, new music can be heard if she listens well enough. She hears music in her mind's ear just like an architect might imagine what a new room in the house might look like in his mind's eye. She works out the sequence of sounds, melodies, harmonies until it satisfies the musical challenge she has set for herself – until she is satisfied that she is done.

The composer is the only one who can hear the musical product until she either performs it herself on a musical instrument or writes the music down in sketch form. For some composers, the act is complete and satisfying without ever hearing the music in the Foreground. Going to the edge of the unconscious and coming back with what they wanted is enough.

For people in business, the process of creating the future is the same, but the medium of expression is different. Creating the future literally means bringing a new future into existence informed by, but not determined by, the past. Business leaders create new futures by imagining valuable business models, new products, new processes, new business relationships, previously unseen synergies, new art and copy for marketing, new possible algorithms for software processes, and so on.

143

Creating the future is the act of imagining something you want to bring into existence that isn't already there and if you don't take action to make it real, it won't happen. You start the process with an intention to manifest something in the world that you really care about. The output of the composing process is a detailed sketch of what will exist in reality when the intended future is present. The question, "What is the intended result?" has been answered at the strategic level. The end of the creative process is when the future you imagined has become real in the Foreground. Creating the future is literally about making dreams come true in reality.

Where Does The Future Exist?

Before a dream becomes a reality, where does it exist? You may be very excited about imagining the new business and how it might be possible. You probably have shared the idea with other people. But until something shows up in the Foreground, it is just an idea. It has no substance. How can the creator get it out of his or her imagination and into reality?

If you think about the past and the future, in what field of existence do they show up? Do they actually exist in reality? Have you ever awakened in the past – woken up and it was yesterday? Not in reality. Have you ever awakened and it was tomorrow and not today? No. In reality, you are always in the present, the Now. But your past and future seem to exist and have impact on your life. So where do they exist? They exist only in language and memory.

The past only exists as story. Your personal past is a collection of your memories from your point of view. The stories that make up your past are repeated, embellished, and eventually become your notion of who you are. You identify so strongly with your personal story that you forget that you constructed it to begin with. The stories that make up the past are stored in Background memory and experienced in Midground recollection. Your past becomes present in your personal reality when it grips you in a PMA or when you focus on it. Your past exists in Foreground reality only when you tell the stories to others.

We know that there is no objective past because people tell different versions of the same shared event. Listening to both sides of a divorce case will make that abundantly apparent. While the facts never change, the narrative that you make of those facts is completely a function of the way you filtered events from your personal point of view. We "objective" observers may never know the facts in full because, as Winston Churchill said, "History is written by the victors."

The future is a possible reality you invent that has no independent existence. At least your past has the advantage of having been repeated over and over until it became who you are. When you wake up in the morning, you don't have to work at keeping your past alive. Your Background programming and the narratives that go with it are automatically there.

The future, on the other hand, requires continual work to keep in existence. Until it becomes real in the Foreground, the future state you intend to create is only an idea that lives in your imagination. Physical work must be done to keep it alive in a world where the past is constantly asserting itself.

145

So in the *Mode of Creation*, you do something quite daring: you imagine a future state that might seem impossible from your actual current state, and then you engage others with language so that they share enthusiasm for your vision. By sharing your vision with others, the future has a larger body of existence. Since it exists only as an inspiring idea expressed in language, the more people who are involved in the discourse, the greater the likelihood of it becoming real.

When enough people are sharing the conversation, the future you are creating becomes an idea whose time has come. The inspiring hope of that possible future lives on in the minds of others beyond its creator.

"One withstands the invasion of armies; one does not withstand the invasion of ideas." – Victor Hugo

Your job as a strategic leader is to create an inspiring future and deliver on it. The first step is to clearly imagine a future that you say is possible, one worth your life energy and precious time, to achieve. The second step is to cause the community that you lead to embrace the idea so that people are inspired to share it with others and to give their own life energy and time to its fulfillment. That is the functional definition of strategic leadership.

How To Advocate for Perennial Values

If you want to move people to share and act on the future you are creating, you must give them a narrative that is vividly detailed enough that they can see, hear, smell, taste, and touch it, now.

146

To get a sense of the power of language to create the sensory presence of something that doesn't exist in current reality, read the following excerpt from a story by Krisha Montmorency.

"After everyone arrived, and the hors d'oeuvre platter was set, Gerry gathered everyone in the dining room for the big moment. "Happy New Year!" he exclaimed as he wound the corkscrew into the top of the bottle. Half of the cork came out while the other half immediately disintegrated into the wine below, and I could feel my stomach sink. Not a good sign. But Gerry, and my dad next to him, were smiling and started laughing like they were kids in a candy shop having a blowout sale.

"Instantly I knew why. Within seconds, on the far side of the room, I was hit straight up the nostrils with the most luxurious and divine smell I had ever encountered in my life. Ten feet away from the bottle! Gerry grabbed a small sieve from the kitchen and began distributing 2-ounce pours of the Sauternes to everyone in his finest, shiniest Riedel crystal Bordeaux glasses. The wine was the color of 24-carat gold, glistening in the light for all to see.

"When my pour came along, I put my nose deep into the glass, inhaled fully, swirled it, and smelled again. I took a sip of the golden elixir and the world stopped. It was the first time in my life where I can recall experiencing genuine tunnel vision. Everything else vanished, nothing else mattered. All that existed was the glass, the wine and me.

"The wine was thick and viscous, beautiful to feel, like drinking silk. It smelled of the earth, vanilla, and oak barrels of a time long gone by. It continued to open and share itself with me as it sat on my tongue. The vapor went up the back of my throat and into my nose once more, and the tastes and

smells of rich honey, spring orange blossom, peach blossom, bursting-ripe peaches, and vanilla-oak surrounded my senses. Along with it was a clean, nuanced sensation of acid, refreshing to my palate. I could barely tell where smelling ended and tasting began. I could feel every empty space inside my head fill itself up with the elegant essence of the wine before me. All that was beautiful and possible in nature, and even humanity itself, was in that glass. I swallowed, and waited. And waited. Thirty seconds. Sixty seconds. The finish was still there! Perfection!

"I closed my eyes and I felt like I was flying. It was nothing less than profound, an experience of the Divine itself."

What images, thoughts, emotions, and sensations came up in your Midground as you read the story? Were you able to taste anything? Did you remember something from your past in the area of family and sharing food? Now, after reading the excerpt, are you interested in tasting wine or dining?

Here is a second example from the political history of the U.S. that is spoken in Mode of Creation language. Note what images, emotions, and body sensations arise as you read this famous excerpt from a transformational time in U.S. history.

"And so even though we face the difficulties of today and tomorrow, I still have a dream. It is a dream deeply rooted in the American dream.

"I have a dream that one day this nation will rise up and live out the true meaning of its creed: 'We hold these truths to be self-evident, that all men are created equal.'

"I have a dream that one day on the red hills of Georgia, the sons of former slaves and the sons of former slave owners will be able to sit down together at the table of brotherhood.

"I have a dream that one day even the state of Mississippi, a state sweltering with the heat of injustice, sweltering with the heat of oppression, will be transformed into an oasis of freedom and justice.

"I have a dream that my four little children will one day live in a nation where they will not be judged by the color of their skin but by the content of their character.

"I have a dream today!

"I have a dream that one day, down in Alabama, with its vicious racists, with its governor having his lips dripping with the words of 'interposition' and 'nullification -- one day right there in Alabama little black boys and black girls will be able to join hands with little white boys and white girls as sisters and brothers.

"I have a dream today!

"I have a dream that one day 'Every valley shall be exalted, and every hill and mountain shall be made low, the rough places will be made plain, and the crooked places will be made straight; and the glory of the Lord shall be revealed and all flesh shall see it together.' This is our hope, and this is the faith that I go back to the South with.

"With this faith, we will be able to hew out of the mountain of despair a stone of hope. With this faith, we will be able to transform the jangling discords of our nation into a beautiful symphony of brotherhood.

"With this faith, we will be able to work together, to pray together, to struggle together, to go to jail together, to stand up for freedom together, knowing that we will be free one day.

"And this will be the day -- this will be the day when all of God's children will be able to sing with new meaning:

"My country 'tis of thee, sweet land of liberty, of thee I sing.
"Land where my fathers died, land of the Pilgrim's pride,
"From every mountainside, let freedom ring!

"And if America is to be a great nation, this must become true. And so let freedom ring from the prodigious hilltops of New Hampshire.

"Let freedom ring from the mighty mountains of New York.

"Let freedom ring from the heightening Alleghenies of Pennsylvania.

"Let freedom ring from the snow-capped Rockies of Colorado.

"Let freedom ring from the curvaceous slopes of California.

"But not only that:

"Let freedom ring from Stone Mountain of Georgia.

"Let freedom ring from Lookout Mountain of Tennessee.

"Let freedom ring from every hill and molehill of Mississippi.

"From every mountainside, let freedom ring.

"And when this happens, when we allow freedom to ring, when we let it ring from every village and every hamlet, from every state and every city, we will be able to speed up that day when all of God's children, black men and white men, Jews and Gentiles, Protestants and Catholics, will be able to join hands and sing in the words of the old Negro spiritual:

"Free at last! Free at last! Thank God Almighty, we are free at last!"

– Dr. Martin Luther King Jr., at the March on Washington, August 28, 1963

What images, thoughts, emotions, and sensations came up in your Midground as you read the speech? What are you feeling now? If you have a full sensation in your chest, you are having the experience of being inspired. The word inspiration comes from the Latin word *spirare*, which means to breathe. When we are inspired, spirit has been breathed into us and we feel that sensation in our chest.

So how does this work? It is nothing short of magical that hearing or reading a string of words can evoke such strong sensations, vivid images, thoughts, and feelings in us. And yet, that is the way that the future is made present by leaders throughout history. New possibilities for life are brought forth in language.

In both examples, the speakers were advocating for universal values that are shared by all people – the values of family and epicurean delight in the first example, and the values of freedom, equality, and brotherhood for all in the second. These are big ideas that resonate with the very best in all of us. Making them present through Mode of Creation speech connects us to the best in ourselves and the best in each other. We are touched and moved to take action to promote those values and the possible future that they make available.

When we are operating in The Mode of Creation we are the most powerful that we can be as human beings. By declaring a future state as possible and vividly creating its presence for others, we begin to manifest that future in reality with high velocity. The more people we can inspire to carry that future, the greater the probability of it coming into physical existence. This is access to real power.

When you speak in the Mode of Creation, your Background intention is to bring a valuable or inspiring possible future into being. When you listen in this mode, your attention is on looking for the details of what is being created. The benefits of operating in this mode are that the speaking is powerfully moving, uplifting, and engages the best in yourself and others. Possible pitfalls of this mode are that speaking in this way can inhibit effective action by making people *feel* that they are making progress when no actual work has been accomplished. It can also provoke cynicism and resistance to the new idea in amounts proportional to the size of the idea – the bigger the possibility, the greater the pushback.

At the mental level, people operating in Creation mode experience a fully integrated flow state with focused presence and quiet mental chatter. The emotions associated with Creation are joy, peace, affinity, and happiness. At the sensory level, people experience a telescoped sense of time, physical relaxation, pleasure, and a strong connection to the body and the Foreground.

Speaking in the Mode of Creation includes advocacy for perennial values, open-ended inquiry into the great questions of life, vivid story telling, and truly creative brainstorming. This is when people actually create rather than rearrange their existing thoughts and prejudices, and show appreciation for others through spontaneous acknowledgments. These are some forms of speech in Creation Mode.

The group effect of communicating in the Mode of Creation is a resilient mood of joy and inspiration where anything seems possible. When people are creating the future together, the effect tends to spiral up and out. The more the future is made present and shared with others, the greater the momentum of high energy and hope and the greater the initiative displayed by the people in the group. This is the opposite of the Mode of Argument where the more you complain and argue, the less power people have and the darker the mood.

Think On This

You can see that making the future present for people on your team is a critically high priority. The most effective way for you to lead your people to deliver on their potentials is to bring into the present an inspiring future that is worth their time and energy to make real.

It only takes one drop of blue ink to change the color of all the water in an aquarium. Take a few minutes each day to share your vision in a vivid and inspiring way with your people.

Insights

Reality Based Leadership

You can now see that your job as a leader is to be a creative artist in the matter of your own life and the future of the community you lead. Your ability to make the future present for those around you is your access to aligning their attentions and inspiring committed action in service to fulfilling that future. It turns out that it doesn't take much time or a lot of work to make the future present. It takes only the courage to speak up and generate a future based conversation in what may be a social milieu where 98% of the time people are presenting their opinions, making complaints, and manipulating each other to get what they want. It is possible to shift people out of their habitual ways of thinking, feeling, and speaking by providing leadership.

At the beginning of this book, we defined leadership as the ability to manifest the leader's intentions in reality with and through people. Now after learning the Modes of Intention, the possibility of building power through the practice of Being Integrated, and having generated insights into your own and others' Background processes, you can see that the medium of leadership is communication. The way we use symbolic, tonal, and gestural language is the access to providing leadership.

Consider the moment-to-moment intentional state of a population working together in an organization. Some are focusing on accomplishing the work in front of them, others are surfing the Web, some are arguing with each other about which is the right next action to take, some are guardedly navigating a difficult conversation with an ineffective manager, and so on. If we took a snapshot of the intentional states of a whole group of people working in an ineffective organization it might look like this.

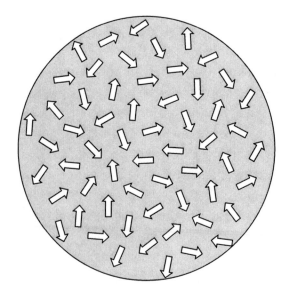

Figure 12: Randomly Unaligned Intentions Inside an Organization

If you grant that the direction of each vector symbolizes the current intent of an individual, you can see that by summing up the vectors the net effect of the aggregate whole is approximately zero movement and indeterminate direction. If there is anything more than Brownian motion of the organization at all it might be caused by exogenous forces. It's basically drifting. This is a model for showing an ineffective organization going essentially nowhere. Corporate leaders often refer to the workforce in organizations like this as "disengaged." There is a lot of "churn" and waste generated, but not much forward progress.

To get the organization to a state of high performance, meaning that it's fulfilling the leader's intentions with high velocity, each individual's intent must be aligned in the same direction. It would look like this.

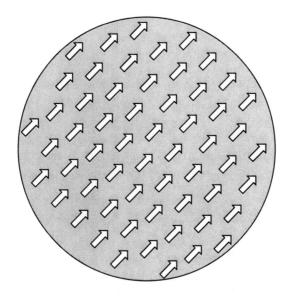

Figure 13: Aligned Intentions Inside an Organization

In this illustration, each person's thoughts, actions, speech, and results are pointing in the same direction – towards the strategic goal. If the vectors are all added up, the net effect is a huge velocity up and to the right. This organization is functioning at high performance.

Another definition of leadership is the ability to align the intentions of a group of people so that their actions fulfill the leader's intended result. Since intentions live in the Background, the skill of leadership involves initiating action by shifting what is in people's Background. If you remember from the chapter on the Source of Power, the domains of human being that are in the Background for almost all people are the Spiritual and Causal domains. They are where our core values, purposes, and intentions live. To align a group of people, a leader must first start with creating an inspiring purpose that all people can share. Leadership is primarily a creative activity.

Strategic Leadership

"Imagination is the beginning of creation. You imagine what you desire, you will what you imagine and at last you create what you will."- George Bernard Shaw

Considering our model for integrity, you can see that powerful action that produces intended results comes from purpose. To align a group of people, the first thing a leader must do is to create a future that can be shared by everyone in the community, a future that is inspiring enough that the group develops a shared purpose.

If, for example, a leader wants to start a community orchestra in a town that has no orchestra, the first job of that leader is to create and articulate a possible future that inspires people enough to want to take action to fulfill that future. The key elements that are required for that future to take hold in the minds and hearts of the people is that it must be considered by everyone to be worth doing and that, most importantly, it is seen as possible. The leader uses love for the possibility and skill in communication to create Creation Mode language that, when heard by people, causes thoughts, images, and emotions to occur in their Midground experience. In a very real sense, the future exists now for the people listening to the leader speak. If bringing an orchestra into existence is viewed by the community as an inspiring and desirable goal, then they will take action to make it happen.

Strategic leadership is composing the future. The action of strategic leadership occurs in the Mode of Creation. Just as a composer of music imagines a beautiful and compelling sequence of sounds that might exist, strategic leaders do the same by imagining a future that might be. In composing, the input is a desire to manifest something in the world that you really want. The output is a sketch of what it might look like in reality.

Once the people have been inspired by the possibility of the future a leader has composed and articulated, they now have a shared purpose and they are aligned in wanting to bring it into existence. Everyone is clear on WHAT he and she will work together to produce. The problem now becomes HOW to coordinate actions and combine skills and abilities to actually accomplish that in reality. This is where many leaders fail. It is relatively easy for some charismatic leaders to imagine a future and even to get people to buy into it. The rub comes when it's time to deliver on it. If the people don't know HOW to get there, the future will never become a reality.

Operational Leadership

> *"People frequently believe the creative life is grounded in fantasy. The more difficult truth is that creativity is grounded in reality, in the particular, the focused, the well observed or specifically imagined."* – Julia Cameron

In the absence of a clear pathway from the current state to the possible future state that has been created, all the inspiration and commitment in the world will not manifest the final result. Results are caused by actions. For a community to coordinate its actions and effectively produce the results that lead to the inspiring future state that is desired requires a clear plan, in fine enough detail to organize and marshal the best that the community has to offer in service of fulfilling its shared purpose. The action of operational leadership occurs in the Mode of Creation.

Going back to our example of the nascent community orchestra, the leader may have successfully inspired the City Council, the local musicians, the volunteer organizations, and the public in the idea of starting the orchestra, but it's all vaporware until people get organized and begin to produce results. Like starting many businesses, starting an orchestra has many moving parts, hundreds of people to lead and organize, loads of equipment, sheet music, and finances to manage, and complex logistics to plan and organize. In the absence of a clear step-by-step plan in time, the first performance may never happen. Or if it does happen, the personal, financial, and social cost of mounting the production could be far more than the community is willing to pay. For the project to turn out, all the moving parts need to be orchestrated in time.

An orchestrator takes the composer's output – the musical sketch – and assigns that basic sequence of notes and harmonies to various instruments. He uses the performing resources at his disposal to embody various parts of the musical idea, fleshing out the basic sketch into a fully realized musical product. So that people can execute the music together, he must give each person in the orchestra exact instructions on when to play, what notes to play, how long and how loud to play, and many other detailed commands. When all these choices are complete, he has expanded the original sketch into a full orchestral score – a precise plan for fifty to one hundred people to execute together in perfect synchronization. Then, each individual person's part is extracted from the plan and printed up as the personal music for which he or she is accountable. Now the whole organization has what they need in detail to be able to execute the music in perfect synchrony.

People in business do orchestration by comparing the current business situation with the imagined desired result and notice what's missing. They then create a step-by-step plan to get from the current state to the desired result, assigning tasks and interim results to the performing resources at their disposal. They plan their own actions and those of others in time, recording their decisions in a project plan. When done well, an operational plan will have enough detail that any person in the organization can see what they are accountable to produce and exactly by when.

In orchestrating, the input is a clearly specified desired result. The output is a detailed plan of who will do what by when and for how much. The question "How will the desired result be produced?" has been answered in detail at the operational level.

So, now the community has a clear pathway that will take them from the current state to the desired future. But a plan is just a plan. It, by itself, causes no results or actions that would produce results. The plan has to be put into action and the interim results produced. This requires leaders to initiate the actions with the performing resources and to oversee the production of the specified results. It requires tactical leaders to execute the plan on time and on budget.

Tactical Leadership

"The great end of life is not knowledge but action."
– Thomas H. Huxley

At this point in the creative process, the community has a shared purpose to fulfill an inspiring future that they view as possible and a clear pathway that makes that future practical and predictable. There are still no results yet in the real world. To execute the planned pathway, tactical leadership is required to coordinate people's intentions that will stimulate the thoughts, emotions, and physical actions that produce tangible results. The action in tactical leadership occurs in the Mode of Execution. Someone needs to tell or ask people what to do and by when to do it.

Some may argue that responsible people will take the plan and execute it themselves through expert collaboration. This may happen, but in systems where there are more than a few players, coordinating communication and actions, resolving the inevitable problems that arise, and adjusting as they go cannot be handled efficiently through self-organization and democratic process. Someone must hold the performers to account for the deliverables to be produced as the plan unfolds. Anyone who has ever accomplished anything complex with a large group of people knows that to be effective requires a central coordinating and synchronizing agency to drive the process – tactical

162

leadership. In the world of large ensemble music making, the conductor provides that function.

A conductor takes the orchestrator's output – a detailed plan containing the exact instructions for each player in the orchestra – and leads the performers in realizing the composer's intentions. Her first job is to become inspired by the composer's vision and intimately familiar with the details of the orchestrator's plan. When her preparation is complete, she goes before the performers in the orchestra and gives precisely detailed verbal and visual directions to them. Because she is a consistently competent leader and has earned the respect of the performers, they willingly execute her directions playing their individual parts in perfect synchronization at the speed directed. In a great orchestra, the players return more than is asked for by adding their own artistic skill and taste to the execution of their part, amplifying the effect of the conductor's direction. The result is greater than the sum of the parts and outperforms the conductor's expectations and, perhaps, the composer's vision.

People in business, when conducting, get inspired by the strategy and operational plan they are executing. They lead and manage their team members with clear communication and consistent focus on the real results. Because they authentically trust and respect their work partners, they are leaders whom others look to for direction and management. They facilitate, teach, direct, train, coach, and lead as required to help others execute the plan in perfect synchronization and harmony.

In conducting, the inputs are a clearly specified result and a detailed plan of action to produce that result. The output of conducting is precisely detailed verbal and visual directions and performance feedback to collaborators who trust, respect, and are willing to follow the conductor. The question "By whom, when, and in what way should this part be played?" is answered fully at the tactical level.

The communication used in actuating the plan is in the Mode of Execution. While some Creation mode speech will be used to set the context and re-presence the future, and some Presentation mode will be required to transfer information, the language that causes action and results is always driven by the Background intention to produce a specific result by a date certain. Someone leading others to deliver results in business will be seen asking and telling people what to do and be making offers of assistance.

Performers as Partners

A performer takes the conductor's directions and applies them to the instructions in his individual part. He is trusted by the conductor and the other members of the orchestra to execute his part at least accurately, and at best, with inspirational skill and style. While he is accountable only for his part, the quality of his work influences the work of others around him in the orchestra. Because he is a trusted partner, rather than a subordinate, he gives feedback and suggests creative solutions to the conductor with the intent to make the performance better for everyone, rather than undermine the conductor's authority.

People in business, when performing, execute the plan on time and on budget, notify managers of bad news early, anticipate problems and provide solutions before the managers know the problems exist. They respectfully say "no" when asked to do things that would make the execution of their primary job impossible. They communicate precisely what they will do by when and reliably do that. If they fail to deliver, they acknowledge the failure and propose a work around. They are responsible owners of the area of the business in which they work.

In performing, the inputs are clear, detailed directions and requests to produce specific measurable results. The outputs are the physical results delivered at the time specified.

Performance Management

When a performer has delivered a result, that product must be assessed to determine if it fulfills the criteria set forth in the operational plan. Does this physical output match the specifications asked for by the tactical leader (the conductor) and increment the community's progress on the pathway to the future? Does it provide value? The role of reviewer is the fundamental function of a manager.

One person may both provide leadership and management, but it is useful to distinguish the functions from one another. One leads people, but manages things. A project manager keeps track of all the commitments that are being delivered upon by a team and assesses with the performers and the tactical leader (perhaps him or herself) the completion of those commitments. A skillful project manager will also remove obstacles, provide resources, and facilitate the performers in executing their accountabilities.

A reviewer audits the results of a performance and assesses the value, beauty, and effect of the composer's vision, the orchestrator's plan, the conductor's leadership and interpretation, and the performer's execution. A reviewer can be any person on the creative team or a customer who is auditing the product. A competent reviewer must base her assessments on the original specifications as given by the composer. The question "Does this performance properly express the composer's original idea?" is answered YES or NO. The reviewer and the creative team acknowledge the result and applause and accolades are given if the answer is YES – explanations and analysis if NO.

Managers in business, when reviewing, compare the specifications for an intended result with the actual result produced. They judge whether or not the actual result fulfills the specifications. The person accountable for the result and the reviewer acknowledge the state of the result and applause and rewards are given if the answer is YES – explanations and analysis if NO. Lessons learned and promises for the future are made.

In reviewing and appreciating, the inputs are the specifications for a desired result and an objective evaluation of the actual result. The outputs are 1) an assessment of satisfactory completion, and 2) appreciation of success or acknowledgment of failure with appropriate consequences for each. The question "Is this the result that was agreed to?" has been answered YES or NO.

Your Job as a Leader

Said simply, your job as a leader is to create and deliver an inspiring future of increasing value by causing effective actions in yourself and others.

There are six activities that, taken together, describe the actions of effective leadership.

1) **Establish a foundation** of mutual respect that connects the group and creates a condition of readiness to perform together.

2) **Compose** and communicate a possible future state that gives the group a shared purpose and the inspiration to fulfill it. (Strategic Leadership)

3) **Orchestrate** a detailed plan of action that gives them a clear pathway that bridges the gap between the current reality and the desired future. (Operational Leadership)

4) **Conduct** coordinated effective action among the performers who are executing the plan. (Tactical Leadership)

5) **Perform** with the performers as the work is accomplished, by removing barriers to effective execution. (Performance in Partnership)

6) **Review and assess** the actual results against the specifications in the operational plan and their value in fulfilling the strategic vision. Acknowledge the results and reward success or mitigate failure leaving the performers whole, empowered, and reengaged in the project. (Performance Management)

These six domains of activity makeup the core of the leadership job. They are provided here as an introduction to the material that will be revealed in depth in the next book of the Leadership, Creativity, and Power series – *Creating the Future*.

Think On This

Consider your own leadership practice in light of the six areas of activity above.

• In the current projects you are leading, which of the areas of activity receives the least attention and energy?

• What are the symptoms of that part of your job not getting done thoroughly?

• What are the deliverables you must provide and the conversations you must have and with whom to bring excellence to that area?

Insights

Insights

Qualifications of a Reality Based Leader

Every job has its required set of knowledge, skills, and abilities that enable the work to get done with ease, effectiveness, and satisfaction. The same is true for the job of leadership. Experience shows that to be effective in the leadership role, you need to be continually developing yourself in five different areas. They are:

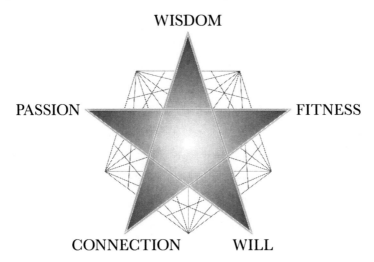

WISDOM

PASSION

FITNESS

CONNECTION

WILL

As a way to close this book and to open another doorway for further progress in your leadership practice, here are the five areas of virtue and the dimensions within them presented as possibilities for you to explore. As you read each section, assess your current level of ability and write down the insights you discover and the actions that you see to take.

1 – Fitness

Fitness is the integral readiness required to lead effectively. Leadership success is always a function of the followers' willingness to entrust their energy and future to the person they've empowered to lead them. Leaders, who are found to be unfit, are at best ineffective at producing high performance in the group and at worst are rejected with prejudice. The three dimensions of fitness for leaders are *stamina, resilience,* and *goodness.*

Stamina is the ability to sustain the output of mental, emotional, and physical energy needed to produce the leadership outcomes required. Your people need you when they need you, not when it suits you. If you expect them to work hard and perform at a high level, you must do the same by example.

Resilience is the ability to recover one's well being quickly after challenges and difficulties. Inevitably in life, circumstances arise that try the strongest of us. Being able to fail after striving to do our best, to succumb to illness or physical trauma, to sustain emotional pain and mental anguish and then bring it all to closure, moving forward unencumbered by the past is a kind of inner toughness that is required of effective leaders.

Goodness is the quality of being in service to the growth, well-being, and integrity of those one leads and of oneself. Those who lead best, lead in a way that makes it seem that those following are creating the success for themselves, by themselves. People thrive in the force field radiated by the leader. The leader considers him or herself as merely a servant fulfilling the shared purpose of the group. If one's actual intent is to gain personally by dominating, manipulating, using, and lying to one's constituents, then that leader is not morally fit to lead. The leader could be described in terms of the opposite of good – evil to a greater or lesser degree.

Honestly assess yourself in the area of Fitness and its constituent virtues – Stamina, Resilience, and Goodness. Ask yourself the following questions.

- Is your current level of ability insufficient or sufficient to provide effective leadership in your current accountability?

- What do you need to do to improve your ability?

- How will you go about it?

- By when will you achieve mastery to your level of satisfaction in the area?

Write down your insights in your insight journal and make commitments to your coach, mentor, or manager to begin developing yourself immediately.

2 – Will

Will is the innate power to intentionally make choices and to act on those choices. Will, in this sense, has been spoken of as spine, gumption, resourcefulness, initiative, nerve, drive, and so on. Your will is what is required to take a stand in the face of resistance and difficult circumstances, and by virtue of that stand, to do the actions required to produce your intended result. The three dimensions of will for leaders are *discipline, technical prowess,* and *courage.*

Discipline is the ability to manage yourself and your actions to reliably produce the results you intend. In reality, the results you produce always correlate to the actions you take in the circumstances. Discipline enables you to take the actions that will likely produce the result you intend. If, for example, you intend to lead people to operate with reliability and integrity, but you yourself are unable to operate with reliability and integrity, then you lack the discipline sufficient to produce that result with your people. Discipline is what it takes to allow yourself to be dominated by your declared purpose, no matter what you feel like at the time.

Technical Prowess is the ability and knowledge to effectively execute the actions required to produce the results you intend to deliver. If you are leading a team of people, but do not know enough about the work they are doing, the technical limitations, the language of the sector you are operating in, and so on, you will not be able to effectively lead them. They will know that you are an impostor. Top performers recognize other top performers. Talking the talk is necessary but insufficient to win the trust of a team of people. Actually walking the walk yourself is required to be an authentic leader. You must have developed the technical prowess to play with the players, or you will not earn the respect of those you lead.

Courage is the ability to take effective action, in spite of your fear, to produce the results you intend. Doing anything challenging, like creating a future that wasn't going to happen by itself, takes courage. Stepping outside the boundaries of the normal causes change, which almost always stimulates the negative emotions of anger and fear in yourself and others. Courage is the virtue that allows you to experience the fear but override your animal self and take the effective action anyway.

Honestly assess yourself in the area of Will and its constituent virtues – Discipline, Technical Prowess, and Courage. Ask yourself the following questions.

• Is your current level of ability insufficient or sufficient to provide effective leadership in your current accountability?

• What do you need to do to improve your ability?

• How will you go about it?

• By when will you achieve mastery to your level of satisfaction in the area?

Write down your insights in your insight journal and make commitments to your coach, mentor, or manager to begin developing yourself immediately.

3 – Connection

Connection is the profound link between people's hearts, minds, and spirits. Human beings are always linked together in all five dimensions (spiritual, causal, mental, emotional, and physical) by gestural, tonal, and symbolic language, and the subtle energies of intentionality and shared purpose. As leaders, we radiate a magnetic field around which our people orient themselves, for better or for worse. The qualities we embody radiate into the environment and influence the intentions, thoughts, feelings, and actions of our people. Our ability to modulate that field connecting us is directly correlated to our ability to lead effectively. The three dimensions of connection for leaders are *appeal, persuasive savvy,* and *communication.*

Appeal is the ability to attract and hold the attention of others in a pleasing and engaging way. To be an effective leader, those who empower you to lead must regard you as worthy of attention and respect. At best, you must be admirable. At worst, you must be at least respectable. Crafting your language, appearance, and style to be simultaneously appropriate, open, and self-authorized is required to gain and retain the attention and respect necessary for leadership to occur.

Persuasive Savvy is the ability to engage and maintain people's support and energy to serve your purpose. As you lead people to fulfill the operational plan to make the future real, they will diverge from the strategic goal. To be effective, you must be able to keep people focused on the goal and handle objections, breakdowns along the way, and challenges that arise from other would-be leaders and unexpected circumstances. Your ability to influence people to change their points of view is a key skill required to keep people on track and continually inspired to fulfill the strategic goal.

Communication is the ability to project your intent by "becoming one together" with your audience. When we speak and listen, the Background intentions driving our experiences and behaviors are expressed into the Foreground. Because of the profound always-existing connection between people, the leader's intentions powerfully shape the intentions of the whole group. Your ability to transparently provide a clear channel to the possibility of the future is your access to having your people communing with each other in service to fulfilling that future.

Honestly assess yourself in the area of Connection and its constituent virtues – Appeal, Persuasive Savvy, and Communication. Ask yourself the following questions.

• Is your current level of ability insufficient or sufficient to provide effective leadership in your current account-ability?

• What do you need to do to improve your ability?

• How will you go about it?

• By when will you achieve mastery to your level of satisfaction in the area?

Write down your insights in your insight journal and make commitments to your coach, mentor, or manager to begin developing yourself immediately.

4 – Passion

Passion is the innate drive to create what you love and continuously improve it. The things we are passionate about call forth from us an almost inextinguishable stream of energy driving what we love into existence. Passion gives us a deep well from which to draw. Passion cannot be faked. The evidence of authentic passion is creative genius striving for excellence in service to a purpose greater than ourselves. The three dimensions of passion for leaders are *creativity, excellence,* and *service.*

Creativity is the ability to imagine and articulate what you want to bring into being. Real creativity can only come from love. When the lower aspects of self can be set aside in favor of humbly listening into the Void, what one loves can sometimes be heard, imagined, and articulated. This way of bringing truly new things into existence is the essence of leadership.

Excellence is the ability to continuously improve one's performance against ever-rising standards. As your skill in leadership improves, the people you lead will rise to the standards you have set for them. What then? When there is no gap between the current reality and the possibility of the future, then there is no structural tension to provide the energy to create, manifest, and deliver. Your ability to apply excellence will enable you to lead your people to the next level in an ongoing way.

Service is the ability to willingly contribute one's energies to a purpose greater than personal benefit. Striving to achieve a personal goal can be motivating on a personal level. It will always be too small, however, to inflame the hearts and minds of others. The ability to serve a purpose greater than oneself is the source of an almost infinite amount of creative energy and inspiration because to serve a Purpose of that magnitude requires that you transcend the imperatives of your animal self. Your people will know whom you serve. If it is the Future, they will give you all that they have.

Honestly assess yourself in the area of Passion and its constituent virtues – Creativity, Excellence, and Service. Ask yourself the following questions.

• Is your current level of ability insufficient or sufficient to provide effective leadership in your current accountability?

• What do you need to do to improve your ability?

• How will you go about it?

• By when will you achieve mastery to your level of satisfaction in the area?

Write down your insights in your insight journal and make commitments to your coach, mentor, or manager to begin developing yourself immediately.

5 – Wisdom

Wisdom is the personal development to fulfill an integrated life. Wisdom is not about acquiring more knowledge. It is about having the complexity of thought needed to see what to do with knowledge. As we develop from children through adolescence, through adulthood into sagacity, our abilities to perceive the greater patterns of things, the meta-systems that drive the surface appearances increase. We call this progression of complexity and perspective the acquisition of wisdom. The three dimensions of wisdom for leaders are *reality awareness, effective prioritization,* and *perspective.*

Reality Awareness is the ability to perceive what's happening with minimal conceptual or sensory distortion. Leaders who respond to the appearance of circumstances that are skewed by their own psychology have a distorted sense of the facts, and often, an emotionally driven response to the situation. Developing the ability to see facts for what they are in a non-personal, amoral context allows for a more rational approach to the situation and a spontaneous creative approach where appropriate. It is impossible to effectively change the circumstances when you can't accurately see what the circumstances are. Distinguishing reality from your ideologies and personal psychology is the key skill here.

Effective Prioritization is the ability to choose what to spend resources on that will make the biggest difference for the whole. Since time and resources are almost always limited, a creative leader grounded in reality will have to make hard choices along the way to fulfilling the future. The ability to discern which actions and decisions will move the plan along the most at a given time is critical to keeping the group and the project on target. When one is leading with clear results and outcomes in mind, sizing up the options at any given point and wisely making the right choice about which path to pursue becomes easier.

Perspective is the ability to see reality from multiple points of view at any altitude. When we are children, our view of the world is constrained by our childish perspective. As we grow and develop, we can imagine what the world must look like for those less developed than us, but we have a hard time imagining what it must look like to those more developed. We have transcended our earlier ways of seeing things, but they are included in our repertoire of possible points of view. As we develop, we continue to transcend and include earlier, less inclusive points of view. It is possible through continual growth and development to see and understand all possible points of view, giving the leader a sympathy and compassion for everyone and allowing for a deep understanding of the Subtle Patterns that underlie all activity.

Honestly assess yourself in the area of Wisdom and its constituent virtues – Reality Awareness, Effective Prioritization, and Perspective. Ask yourself the following questions.

• Is your current level of ability insufficient or sufficient to provide effective leadership in your current accountability?

• What do you need to do to improve your ability?

• How will you go about it?

• By when will you achieve mastery to your level of satisfaction in the area?

Write down your insights in your insight journal and make commitments to your coach, mentor, or manager to begin developing yourself immediately.

For some of the virtues described above, you may assess yourself as insufficiently able to meet your current leadership accountabilities. That is good news, because it gives you a place to start to develop yourself to the next level. Like hiking up a mountain with no summit, leadership is a path of mastery that can be followed throughout life. Who you are has a potential for the awakening and greatness of others in an infinite progression into your own awakening and greatness.

★

Think On This

As you begin to develop your leadership ability to the next level, some practices you can adopt will powerfully accelerate your progress.

1) ***Start practicing serious meditation.*** Sitting for a few minutes each day to reduce stress or to focus your attention is a great place to start. If you wish to accelerate your development in Reality Based Leadership, however, beginning to practice meditations from the ancient wisdom traditions is highly recommended. Hindu, Buddhist, Christian, Sufi, Taoist, and other traditions provide time tested, highly effective, "industrial strength" technologies for expanding the complexity of your awareness and thereby your ability to see and understand the Subtle Patterns and multiple points of view of the people you lead and compete with. Find a certified teacher/trainer and begin to develop your inner leader.

2) ***Sleep more, consume less.*** The one thing you can do to increase your fitness to lead most is to get eight hours of sleep every night. Sleep has a profound effect on your well being impacting your resilience, your stamina, and your clarity of thought and emotional stability. Overwork, over-worry, and over-busyness are symptoms of a life that is fragmented. Do what it takes to take control of your daily experience. Stop chasing things and status; start chasing what gives you health, well-being, and joy. The magnetic field you radiate into your organization will shift dramatically for the good, and you will find that all those things you wanted will appear as a by product of your causing those around you to thrive.

3) *Pay attention.* Notice the modality of speech of the conversations you engage in. Listen skillfully to yourself to see the Modes in action. With practice, you will be able to see how you use Pretense, Argument, and Presentation in normal conversations. As you begin to observe what's driving your behavior, by extension, you will be able to ascertain what is driving the behaviors of others. When you can hear what's going on in the Background of a conversation, you have an opening to intervene and shift the Mode.

4) *Provide leadership.* When you are in a meeting that is going nowhere, listen for the opportunity to intervene in the counterproductive conversation. Following many minutes of analysis, reporting, or arguing, a skillfully made request or offer can shift the modality of everyone's thinking. We have one precious life (that we know of). Don't let people waste your time, and help them to not waste their own.

5) *Be appropriate.* If you are connected to the reality of the present, and you have the intention to create a great future in service to something other than yourself, you will likely appear to normal people as somewhat unusual. To make this a good thing, always pay attention to what you are leaving people with. After meeting with you, if people walk away inspired and engaged, with respect for you and what you stand for, then you are getting your job done as a leader. If they leave you thinking that you are eccentric, brusque, impolite, a crazy visionary, or an enthusiastic but impractical dreamer, you have not connected with them in a way that they find appropriate from their point of view.

6) ***Stop working on solving problems.*** The supply of them is infinite. Start living from the future you are creating and inspire others to do so as well. You'll see that your problems will disappear in your experience and become only things to accomplish.

7) ***Stop tolerating suffering in yourself and others.*** If you are suffering, it's because you are having an Argument with Reality or you have been taken over by your psychology. Do what you need to do to bring unresolved issues and relationships from the past to a close. Communicate with people to give thanks, express gratitude, ask for forgiveness, and to forgive. Complete your last will, pay your back taxes, clean up the garage… put your life in order. The weight it will lift from you will be transformational. Help others to do the same.

Insights

Insights

Afterword

Being a person who is willing to engage in personal growth and development in service to a purpose higher than your own advantage is a noble and valuable calling. The world needs more of you. The author's life purpose is to evoke, communicate, and manifest truth, beauty, and goodness with those who are ready to do the work. If you find that you are ready, training in Leadership, Creativity, and Power mindware may be your next step.

To conclude, here are some inspiring words from Sir Edmund Hillary's speech on the power of commitment:

> *"Until one is committed, there is hesitancy, the chance to draw back, always ineffectiveness, concerning all acts of initiative (and creation). There is one elementary truth the ignorance of which kills countless ideas and splendid plans: that the moment one definitely commits oneself, then Providence moves too. All sorts of things occur to help one that would never otherwise have occurred. A whole stream of events issues from the decision, raising in one's favor all manner of unforeseen incidents and meetings and material assistance which no man could have dreamed would have come his way. 'Whatever you can do or dream you can, begin it. Boldness has genius, power and magic in it. Begin it now.'"* [3]

---

3 Couplet attributed to Johann Wolfgang von Goethe

Acknowledgments

This book is the result of many gifts; the kindness, generosity, grace, and persistence of hundreds of people who have been my friends and mentors throughout my life. The ideas in the book are an evolutionary synthesis of decades of meditation, community service, training, creative art making, engineering, business failures and successes, relationships, and personal growth. None of that would have happened without a supportive community of friends and mentors too numerous to be fully listed here. If you are one of those, know that I am eternally grateful for the gifts you have given me or allowed me to give you on the way to contributing this set of ideas.

Special thanks go to Seth Taube for giving me the freedom to create this book. Also to be thanked are Jubal Raffety and Samuel Jones who, because of their commitment to my success, showed me that I could be an effective leader in spite of my Background programming. I thank the great spiritual teachers Charan Singh Maharaj, Werner Erhard, Irving Fuerst, and all their followers who taught me the ways of the Subtle Power.

Finally, I am grateful to my patient, creative, and loving wife Krisha, for her unflagging support throughout this project.

Gabriel Sakakeeny
San Francisco, CA

About the Author

Gabriel Sakakeeny is the President and Chief Technology Officer of LUMENT, a San Francisco-based human effectiveness technology provider. He started his career in the audio technology space as an electronic engineer, eventually becoming the VP R&D/Manufacturing for Precision Fidelity. In a career-changing move, he won full scholarships to the Juilliard School, the San Francisco Conservatory of Music, and Rice University to study orchestral leadership. After taking his Master's Degree at Rice University, he won the position of Music Director and Principal Conductor of the Houston Youth Symphony and the Houston Youth Ballet from an international field of over 200 hopefuls.

In 1990, Sakakeeny co-founded Jupiter Systems (now Antares Audio Technologies), a software company specializing in advanced signal processing applications for audio, and served there as CEO for 5 years. After exiting Jupiter Systems, he worked as a leadership development consultant, trainer, and executive coach. He joined Agilent Technologies in 1999, where he led an overall corporate change initiative that transformed the culture of the company and produced breakthrough business results in the wake of the telecom crash.

During this same period, Sakakeeny founded and served as president of the American Philharmonic Association for 13 years. In 2010, the Chinese government sponsored American Philharmonic on an eight-city tour of China under Sakakeeny's artistic leadership. In 2011, he was awarded Special Congressional Recognition from the United States Congress for his work with American Philharmonic as a conductor, cultural ambassador, and community leader. He continues to serve as the Music Director Emeritus of the American Philharmonic.

Sakakeeny possesses a unique body of experience focused on leading people and organizations to produce extraordinary results and high performance. This combined work, life experience, and research has enabled his authorship of the book *Subtle POWER* and the Leadership, Creativity, and Power mindware. In both, he delivers a unique and practical method for dramatically improving the ways people work together. This system yields consistently measurable and sustainable improvements in business performance and employee attitude across cultures, ages, and genders around the world.

Find Out More

Exposing yourself to the ideas in this book may have inspired you to begin developing yourself in the discipline of Leadership, Creativity and Power. If you are interested in training in this art form or you see that introducing these ideas to your workforce is a next step for your team, please visit www.lument.co for more information on how to proceed.

Other books in the Leadership, Creativity, and Power series will be published soon. If you wish to be notified of their availability, please send your request to LCPBook@ lument.co. You will be notified when they become available.

Index

K

L

M

N

O

P

W

CPSIA information can be obtained at www.ICGtesting.com
Printed in the USA
LVOW07*1217160915

454302LV00001B/5/P